RACE, CRIME, AND CRIMINAL JUSTICE

Perspectives in Criminal Justice 2

ABOUT THE SERIES

The *Perspectives in Criminal Justice* series is designed to meet the research information needs of faculty, students and professionals who are studying and working in the field of criminal justice. The *Series* will cover a wide variety of research approaches and issues related to criminal justice. The books are collections of articles not previously published, and each book will focus on specific themes, research topics, or controversial issues.

The articles selected for publication are revised versions of papers presented at the annual meetings of the Academy of Criminal Justice Sciences. Papers organized around a specific topic are reviewed by the book's editor and a panel of referees for comment and suggestions for revision. The *Series* will rely on a multidisciplinary approach to such topical areas as organizational theory and change, the nature of crime, law and social control, and applied research as well as the traditional areas of police, courts, corrections, and juvenile justice.

The current volumes include:

- *Corrections at the Crossroads: Designing Policy*, edited by Sherwood E. Zimmerman and Harold D. Miller
- *Race, Crime, and Criminal Justice*, edited by R. L. McNeely and Carl E. Pope

Comments and suggestions from our readers are encouraged and welcomed.

Series Editor
John A. Conley
Criminal Justice Program
University of Wisconsin—Milwaukee

Race, Crime, and Criminal Justice

Edited by
R. L. McNeely
and Carl E. Pope

SAGE PUBLICATIONS   Beverly Hills   London

For information address:

SAGE Publications, Inc.
275 South Beverly Drive
Beverly Hills, California 90212

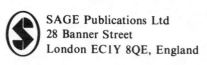

SAGE Publications Ltd
28 Banner Street
London EC1Y 8QE, England

Printed in the United States of America

Library of Congress Cataloging in Publication Data

Main entry under title:
Race, crime and criminal justice.

    (Perspectives in criminal justice; v. 2)
    "Published in cooperation with the Academy of Criminal Justice Sciences."
    Bibliography: p.
    1. Crime and criminals—United States—Addresses, essays, lectures. 2. Race—
Addresses, essays, lectures. 3. Criminal justice, Administration of—United States—
Addresses, essays, lectures.
I. McNeely, R. L. II. Pope, Carl E. III. Academy of Criminal Justice Sciences. IV. Series.
HV6197.U5R33   364'.089   80-28347
ISBN 0-8039-1584-5   AACRI

ISBN 0-8039-1585-3 (pbk.)

FIRST PRINTING

CONTENTS

I. INTRODUCTION   7

1. Race, Crime, and Criminal Justice: An Overview
    Carl E. Pope and R. L. McNeely   9

II. RACE-RELATED PROBLEMS AND CRIMINAL
    JUSTICE: TWO EXAMPLES   29

2. Socioeconomic and Racial Issues in the Measurement
    of Criminal Involvement
       R. L. McNeely and Carl E. Pope   31
3. Spanish-Speaking People and the North American
    Criminal Justice System
       Bonnie J. Bondavalli and Bruno Bondavalli   49

III. EMPIRICAL EXAMINATION OF RACIAL BIAS   71

4. Parole Decision Making and Native Americans
       Tim Bynum   75
5. Race and Extreme Police-Citizen Violence
       James J. Fyfe   89
6. Black and White Violent Delinquents:
    A Longitudinal Cohort Study
       Richard L. Schuster   109
7. Juvenile Court Dispositions of Status Offenders:
    An Analysis of Case Decisions
       William Feyerherm   127

IV. PROPOSALS FOR CHANGE: TWO EXAMPLES   145

  8. Community Justice Versus Crime Control
      Philip Parnell   147
  9. Criminology and Criminal Justice Education in
      Historically Black Colleges and Universities
      Julius Debro   161

About the Authors   175

I.

Introduction

RACE, CRIME, AND CRIMINAL JUSTICE:
An Overview

Carl E. Pope and R.L. McNeely

University of Wisconsin —Milwaukee

Before undertaking an examination of various issues dealing with race, crime and criminal justice, there are a number of factors that should be considered by the reader. The purpose of this brief overview is to highlight some of those factors in order to help place this collection of readings in perspective. We begin by documenting the increasing concern of citizens with crime and its control noting both official and academic responses to this concern. We argue that the major "crime control perspective" is conservative, if not reactionary, in nature and also that it is race specific. Much of the available data, although questionable, shows that Blacks and other minority groups are overrepresented in official counts of crime and delinquency. These data are often accepted unquestioningly as factual and, hence, guide both public perception and policy regarding the problem of crime. Further, both historical and current theoretical speculation perpetuates a racially distorted perspective. Similarly, much of that research focusing upon race and crime is ambiguous and contradictory in nature even with the advent of more sophisticated research methodologies and attention to the inadequancies of earlier studies. We do note, however, some important new research findings focusing upon such factors as "accumulated disadvantaged status" and the role of organizational factors in criminal justice decision making. These lines of inquiry should prove promising in the future and aid in our understanding of a critical social problem.

CONCERN WITH CRIME AND CRIMINAL JUSTICE

Over the past two decades, the American public has become increasingly concerned with the problem of crime and its control. Results of Gallup, Harris, Roper, and other opinion polls tallying public attitudes have reflected this increased concern. In one recent Gallup survey, for example, crime was listed as a major social problem of those residing in cities of over 500,000 population—21% of those queried mentioned crime as among the more pressing social issues affecting their lives. In a similar Gallup poll conducted in 1949, only 4% of the respondents mentioned crime as a major social problem. Further, surveys dealing with criminal justice issues reveal that the bulk of the population favors a more punitive stance toward law violators (Hindelang, 1975). This is particularly true with regard to death penalty legislation for which public support has risen dramatically over the past few years. While 53% of all respondents favored capital punishment for persons convicted of murder in 1972, this figure rose to 67% in 1977. Similarly, 66% of the public felt that the courts are not harsh enough with criminals in 1972 compared to 83% in 1977 (Parisi et al., 1979: 321, 326).

A corollary of the public's concern for crime and a conservative ideology of crime control has been a high level of fear of criminal victimization, especially among the elderly. A 1975 survey conducted by the National Council on the Aging revealed that of those elderly persons 65 years of age and over, 23% reported fear of crime as a major social problem (National Council on Aging, 1975). Further, elderly citizens frequently express fear at being outside of their homes during both daylight and night-time hours. Other population segments have also expressed high levels of fear of victimization especially with regard to their personal safety on or about the streets at night. For example, as an aggregate figure, 45% of the population surveyed in 1977 expressed fear at walking alone at night in their own neighborhood. Further, in 13 survey cities, 87% of the respondents thought that other people have limited or changed their activities because of crime. Forty-nine percent of those surveyed reported actually having changed or limited their own activities because of crime. (Parisi et al., 1979: 288, 292, 293).

Available data indicate that public concern with rising crime and fear of being victimized are not unwarranted. The Uniform Crime Reports (UCR) of the Federal Bureau of Investigation have shown a startling increase in criminal arrests over the past two decades especially for crimes against the person. During the period from 1946 to 1964, the recorded rates of violent crime rose from 1.1 to 1.3 incidents per thousand persons in the population. However, between 1964 and 1975 the rate of violent crime per thousand reached a high of 4.8, or a 336% increase. Similar trends are also noted for property offenses. The burglary rate alone increased by 500% from 1946 to 1975 (Skogan, 1979). From 1967 to 1976 the percent of all arrests increased by 20.9 percentage points; this included a 36.4% increase in arrests of those under 18 years of age and a 16.1% increase for those 18 years of age and older. In the same period, violent crime increased by 71.7% compared to a 65.7% increase for property crime (Parisi et al., 1979: 481). Trends with regard to collective violence have also been dramatic especially during the 1960s. Generally speaking, violence in the United States has been more widespread and intense when compared to most other Western democratic countries (Gurr, 1979). As Radzinowicz and King point out, the problem of crime is international in scope.

> No national characteristics, no political regime, no system of law, police, justice, punishment, treatment, or even terror has rendered a country exempt from crime. In fact, scarcely anyone can claim to have checked its accelerating momentum. The incidence seems to be going up in all parts of the world, whatever the stage of development and among all segments of society; the previously law-abiding as well as the previously criminal. New forms of crime are emerging and old forms are assuming new dimensions [1977: 3].

RESPONSES TO CRIME

Within this country the official response to these trends has been equally dramatic as witnessed by the proliferation of national, state, and local investigatory commisions; the number of recommendations about major changes necessary in crime control strategies; and the responses of government officials in proposing and enacting legislation aimed at supposed solutions to the crime problem. Initial government response has generally been in the direction of increased federal spending for crime control under the Omnibus Crime Control and Safe Streets Act of 1968 and other legislation. Most of these funds have been spent on the development and dissemination of police "hardware" to supress outbursts of collective violence (mostly ghetto riots) and street crime. Another approach begun in the late 1960s has been the development of computerized data systems to improve criminal justice efficiency. Among such national systems are included: Standardized Crime Reporting System (SCRS); Attribute Based Reporting System (ABRC); Computerized Criminal Histories (CCH); National Trial Court Information System (GRAVEL); Prosecution Management Information System (PROMIS); State Judicial Information System (SJIS); Offender-Based Transaction Statistics (OBTS); and Offender-Based State Corrections Information Systems (OBSCIS). While the above data systems have supported some social science research efforts, the primary thrust has been toward crime control.

Aside from increased expenditures and the development of sophisticated data systems, the major policy thrust in the last decade has been conservative in nature, focusing upon street crime arising from inner-city neighborhoods. This trend can be seen in the continuing transition from indeterminate to fixed sentencing statutes, the increase in death penalty legislation, various restrictions on access to bail coupled with an increase in preventive detention proposals, increased prison construction, an emphasis on retribution, and the like. Similarly, many of the constitutional safeguards enumerated by the Warren Court have gradually been eroded by the more conservative stance of the current Supreme Court. "Tough on crime" and "law and order" slogans serve as political rhetoric for a more conservative and repressive stance with regard to criminal justice. For example, Senate Bill 1722 (a reworked version of the infamous Senate Bill 1) proposes a major revamping of the federal criminal code which substantially broadens many criminal justice procedures while severely limiting traditional constitutional safeguards. In this regard, S.1722 incorporates a variety of provisions to circumvent the prescribed *Miranda* warnings and to allow judges to deny bail and imprison accused persons before trial. In the area of criminal sentencing, S.1722 proposes high maximum penalties and fines and requires mandatory minimum sentences in certain cases. In effect, it provides for a determinate sentencing system, eliminates parole boards, and severely limits early-release options. Much of the current proposed changes in state legislative codes is consistent with above-noted trends in the federal criminal justice system.

Academics have also been attentive to the crime problem. In the last decade there has been a marked increase in the number of journal articles dealing with crime-related issues and a proliferation of journals specifically devoted to criminal justice. It is also during this time period that "criminal justice" emerged as a separate and distinct field of study. The growing body of criminal justice research has focused upon a variety of diverse topics ranging from the deterrent effects of punishment to the disutility of rehabilitative programming. Much of this research has proven to be ambiguous, contradictory, and controversial in nature. For example, a continuous series of debates have centered upon the importance of policy-focused research versus etiological research. Wilson (1975) has argued that continuing efforts to understand the causes of crime are futile because they have no direct policy implications. Emphasis, therefore, should shift toward the development of workable strategies that would impact directly upon the crime problem. Similarly, a group of "neoconservative" academicians have emerged who argue for more punitive responses to crime and criminals. The writings of these intellectuals often serve as political and ideological justification for more repressive government crime control policies (Platt and Takagi, 1977).

RACE AS A FACTOR IN CRIME AND CRIMINAL JUSTICE

Within the United States, the increasing rate of crime and criminal victimization (and, hence, public perception and government policy) is race specific. Reliance upon the UCR and other official data to investigate the relationship between race and crime has overwhelmingly pointed to the disproportionate number of black arrests. Further, this finding has been quite consistent over the past four decades (Pope, 1979). In sum, while it has been estimated that Blacks make up approximately 11% of the United States population (based upon the 1970 census), when aggregated across all offense categories, Blacks constitute 26% of all recorded arrests. This disproportionate arrest rate is substantially higher for crimes of violence compared to property offenses (Skogan, 1979). Although less comprehensive, similar patterns are observed for other racial minorities as well. With regard to American Indians, Stewart (1964), utilizing UCR data, discovered that their arrest rate was three times that of Blacks and eight times that of whites. Further, the public disorder crime of drunkenness accounted for 71% of all American Indian arrests. In a replication of Stewart's earlier study, Reasons (1972) found similar trends in that American Indians were substantially overrepresented in arrest figures. For alcohol-related offenses. Reasons found the arrest rate of American Indians to be eight times that of Blacks and 20 times that of whites. Since the UCR does not distinguish Hispanic persons in their arrest data, national trends are difficult to establish. Nevertheless, available state data indicate that Hispanic persons account for a disproportionately large volume of prison populations (Moore, 1978). Thus, when using arrest, conviction, or prison statistics as a measure of crime, racial minorities are found to be significantly involved in criminal activity.

Perceptions Regarding Race and Crime

While the validity of official and other data sources as estimates of minority involvement in crime has been questioned (McNeely and Pope, 1978), such data are likely to shape public perception and underscore various criminal justice policy decisions. This was graphically illustrated in the aftermath of social protest and ghetto riots of the 1960s. Large-scale racial protest and resulting violence was often viewed as irrational, unjustified, and unique in American history. Both participants and nonparticipants in riot-torn cities were frequently met with repressive state action (Balbus, 1973; Button, 1978). Federal assistance to local police and reaction to possible riot conditions were generally conservative in nature in an attempt to maintain law and order at any cost. Relatively little effort was made to ameliorate discriminatory social and economic conditions (Button, 1978). Thus, both official and unofficial rationalizations for, and reactions to, riot conditions tended to support the status quo. Other explanations that did not conform to the traditional viewpoints were ignored.

It has been rather well-documented that black protest frequently generated into large-scale violence as a direct result of police action (Kritzer, 1977). For example, Hahn and Feagin (1970) argue that every major incident of urban violence that occurred during the 1960s was triggered by police violence. This position is well-summarized by Brown:

> Police brutality, police riots (in which large numbers of police rage out of control in a law-enforcement situation, as happened in Chicago at the 1968 Democratic National Convention) and the violence in penal institutions, all illustrate the paradoxical but intimate and all too common, connection between lawfulness and lawlessness [1979: 31].

From another perspective, collective ghetto violence may be seen as a rational response to an irrational system that excludes Blacks and other minorities from full participation. Such exclusion has traditionally been found in discriminatory processes existing within various social institutions such as schools, churches, businesses, and the like. Unfortunately, such perspectives are often ignored in attempting to understand collective and individual instances of minority crime.

Theoretical Perspectives

Popular accounts of why Blacks and other minority groups engage in collective violence and are thought to be overrepresented in crime counts range from the conditions of poverty, lack of educational opportunities, the history of brutality and subjugation, unemployment, social and legal discrimination, and similar factors. Although such factors have often been incorporated in etiological theories of race and crime, they have not been consistent and well-integrated. Further, research focusing on such factors and more general theoretical speculation has been contradictory and ambiguous. This, in part, stems from a number of interrelated factors. Most of the major theories purporting to understand the relationship between race and crime are so broad in nature that they fail to explain individual differences. Similarly, most major sociological theories have been unable to provide a direct link to the propositions derived from them. The methodology typically employed to establish a causal connection among such factors has generally ignored the perspective of minority group members (Woodson, 1977) and has typically been biased in attending to crime in the lower classes (Thio, 1973). Such conceptualizations often serve to reinforce existing stereotypes (Liazos, 1972). Further, most research efforts dealing with race and crime have made comparisons between minority and majority group members. Few studies have made within-group comparisons focusing on differences and similarities between those who violate the law and those who do not. With some notable exceptions (Curtis, 1975; Silberman, 1978) there have been relatively few studies that have directly attempted to examine causal factors in minority crime. The following observation made by Sellin (1939) over four decades ago probably is still accurate today.

It is unfortunate that belief in the Negro's excessive criminality has made students of Negro crime expend so much energy in attempts to verify the charge. Attention has thus been diverted from much more fundamental matters, such as the causes of crime and the relationship of the Negro to our agencies of justice.

In sum, the "poverty" of both current theory and research has, for the most part, encumbered any real understanding of the possible linkages between race and crime.

Any consideration of the relationship between race and crime must consider a number of issues from both a historical and contemporary perspective. For example, there is the political context of the term *race*. This term has invariably been utilized in a biological and sociological sense. It is interesting to note, however, that the concept of race originated as political justification for subjugation of various ethnic groups in continental Europe and elsewhere during the 18th century. As noted above, the political context of "race and crime" was again demonstrated in the aftermath of the major ghetto riots of the 1960s (Button, 1978). It was only during the latter part of the 19th century that the concept began to take on a biological orientation which, in turn, led to the development of various social eugenics movements and the idea of "racial" superiority and inferiority. It should be noted that biologically there are more similarities than differences among various racial groups. In a sociological sense, the concept invites in-group and out-group feelings which are frequently used as justification for racist practices whether institutional, collective, or individual.

Further, in order to adequately study race and crime, one must understand the process of subjugation of all racial minorities in this country. From a historical standpoint, subjugation often took three distinct forms—slave transfers, colonization, and importation. Slave transfers involved complete subjugation of one racial stock and their transfer to another country for slave labor. The classic example in the United States has been the appropriation of Black Africans. In the second form, an indigenous racial group is subjugated by a nonindigenous group. American Indians have been the primary victims of colonization as well as Hispanics in the southwestern part of the United States. The importation of racial and ethnic groups to supplement available labor has also been used in this country as a form of subjugation. In the 1800s, Chinese and Irish laborers were imported to help build the transcontinental railway system, often working under subhuman conditions for barely subsistence wages. In a modern form of importation, large numbers of Hispanics annually cross into this country for minimal agricultural jobs in California and other border states. Subjugation and racial distinction has frequently led to a differentiation of social services provided to population segments. A good example is provided in the area of mental health care. Grob notes that as mental institutions developed in this country, they frequently provided different services to different populations.

In general, the best care was given native-born paying patients. On a descending scale, they were followed by Native-born poor and indigent patients, and below them were poor and indigent immigrants. At the bottom were blacks, who received the lowest quality of care [Grob, 1973: 223].

While historical modes of subjugation were more blatant and insidious, modern forms of subjugations still exist in the ecomonic, social, political, and legal sectors often leading to discriminatory treatment.

Selection Bias and Related Research

Within the criminal justice system, it has frequently been argued that racial minority offenders receive substantially different treatment than majority offenders. In 1972, a majority of the U.S. Supreme Court, in a 5-to-4 decision, ruled that the death penalty, as then administered, constituted cruel and unusual punishment (*Furman v. Georgia*, 92 S.Ct. 2726). Aside from its landmark stature as a frontal attack on death penalty legislation, *Furman* is important from an additional perspective. As noted in the majority decision, the Court officially underscored the possibility of discrimination in the imposition of the death penalty. The decision to invoke the death penalty, whether made by judge or jury, is a sentencing decision. That such a decision is often made in a capricious and arbitrary manner struck the majority of the Court as inherently unfair. Justice Stewart, for example, observed that the death penalty has often been imposed disproportionately on Blacks and other minority groups and that selection bias based upon race is constitutionally unpermissible.

The charge of racial discrimination raised by the *Furman* decision can also be applied to other stages of the criminal justice system. While the available research literature examining selection bias based upon race by

police, court, and correctional officials has not yielded consistent findings, overall, these results are cause for concern. Much of the earlier
research regarding racial differences focused upon an examination of
sentencing differentials or, more specifically, sentence length. One of the
earliest empirical assessments of differential sentencing practices was a
study conducted in North Carolina, Georgia, and Virginia by Johnson
(1941). For the period 1930 to 1940, this study did find evidence of
differential sentencing for black offenders especially those who had killed
whites. Garfinkle (1949) replicated Johnson's study with similar results—
black offenders were treated more severely than white offenders. Bullock
(1941) and Vines and Jacobs (1963) also examined sentencing data which
supported the existence of differential treatment for black offenders.
Bensing and Schroeder (1960) and Green (1961, 1964), however, could
find no evidence of discriminatory sentencing practices when relevant
control variables were introduced.

A variety of attempts have been made to account for the contradictory
findings such as those noted above. Hindelang (1969), for example, reviewed discrimination, the data were drawn from southern jurisdictions, the
data were older (by approximately 10 years), the focus was on violent
offenses (generally capital cases), and relevant control variables were not
introduced. Hagan (1972), in a similar survey, noted that statistically
significant relationships indicating racial bias in eight studies had no
substantive meaning in that the correlation coefficients were weak. Hagan
did note, however, that four out of five studies focusing on interracial
capital crime showed evidence of racial disparity. More recently, Cohen
and Kluegel (1978) have argued that those researchers finding evidence of
racial bias in juvenile processing have lacked sophisticated methodological
designs which simultaneously control for legal factors. In their own dispositional study of juvenile court processing in Denver, Colorado, and
Memphis, Tennessee, Cohen and Kluegel utilized Goodman's method of
log-linear analysis and could find no evidence of race or social class bias
after appropriate control variables were introduced. Finally, it has been
noted that much of the research literature examines only one decision
point in criminal processing (or one indicator of severity), thus ignoring
the dynamic aspects of the criminal justice system (Pope, 1976).

While much of the more recent research examining racial biases utilizes
multiple decision points, uses more current data, attends to both statistical
and substantive significance, and is generally more methodologically rigor-
ous, contradictory findings are still forthcoming. As noted above, Cohen
and Kluegel (1978, 1979) could find no evidence of race or class discrimi-

nation in juvenile processing when legally relevant variables were appropriately controlled for. Similarly, Burke and Turk (1975), Moore and Roesti (1980), Dagher (1975), Dison (1976), Sutton (1975), Lizotte (1978), and others found no direct evidence of race discrimination. Yet, there is a growing body of research which demonstrates that offender and/or victim race may influence judicial decision making.

Hall and Simkus (1975), in comparing sentencing patterns of American Indians and whites, discovered that the former were more likely to receive a sentence involving incarceration. These authors argue that an offender's attitude and probation officer recommendations may have a substantial impact on differential sentencing outcomes. Thomas and Cage (1977) examined juvenile cases processed by one metropolitan court between January 1, 1966, and July 31, 1973. Controlling for offense type and prior offense record, they found that black offenders were treated more harshly than white offenders. Thornbury (1973), Foley and Rasche (1979), Meyers (1979), Farrell and Swigert (1978), Uhlman (1979), and others have also demonstrated racial differences in criminal justice decision making. However, Frazier and Hernetta (1980) found substantial evidence of a direct race effect in criminal sentencing concluding:

> Race bias may enter the criminal justice process early and be passed on in the form of sentencing recommendations on the pre-sentence report. This suggests race bias may be passed on subtly through recommendations for sentence as well as through formal decisions such as arrest charges, bail dispositions, charges on an indictment, or the charges finally accepted in guilty pleas.

Methodological Issues

Recent examinations of the more covert aspects of criminal justice decision making have provided some support for the above premise. For example, while the bulk of research on police discretion has focused upon arrest decisions, there are a variety of other highly discretionary police decisions in which extralegal factors may play a prominant role. In crimes of a personal nature, Cordner et al. (1980) found that police investigative effort was most strongly associated with the employment status of the victim. For property offenses, however, police investigative effort was influenced by the amount of the evidence present. Also, employed victims were likely to accrue greater investigatory effort while Blacks were less likely to have their cases investigated. Hepburn (1977) demonstrated that non-whites compared to whites were more likely to be arrested under circumstances that would not constitue sufficient ground for prosecution. This relationship was found to vary depending upon the seriousness of the offense and racial composition of the population residing within the precinct area. In examining postarrest police dispositions to release burglary arrestees, Pope (1978) found that such decisions were influenced by nonlegal factors including race, when legal factors were absent. Holland and Johnson (1979) found ethnic differences in sentence recommendations depending upon whether the decision maker was a clinician or caseworker. Whites received relatively lenient case dispositions compared to Mexican American and Black offenders based upon the recommendation of caseworkers. Meyers and Hagan (1979), in examining prosecutional decisions to prosecute a case, found racial effects favoring whites when the strength of the evidence was held constant.

The aggregation and disaggregation of data may also play an important role in discovering racial differences in criminal processing. In examining superior court decisions in Fulton County, Altanta, Gibson (1978) showed that when the data were aggregated across all judges, the court did not appear to discriminate against Blacks. However, in examining individual patterns of judicial decision making, evidence of racial discrimination was apparent. Further, the variance in discriminating sentences among judges could best be accounted for by their backgrounds and attitudes. Gibson (1978) underscores the importance of attending to such methodological issues because improper conclusions may easily be drawn when appropriate control variables and levels of analysis are not utilized. Zingraff and Thomson (1979) examined dispositional outcomes for all males sentenced in North Carolina to an active prison term for armed robbery for the years 1969, 1973, and 1977. If the data are aggregated for the three years, legal factors are most pronounced and there is little evidence of racial disparity. However, separate analysis by year reveals a direct and independent relationship between race and sentence length for the year 1977.

Another important perspective in examining race differences is the role of "accumulated disadvantaged status." In essence, this incorporates a process by which initial differential decisions become amplified as one moves through the criminal justice system. As Farrell and Swigert note in their study of intergroup and intragroup homicides:

> The institutionalization of criminal conceptions in the legal system implies that the administration of justice is an interpretive process.

At each stage, legal representatives assess the offender and the offense that official sanction is warranted. From arrest through final conviction and sentencing, these assessments are guarded, in part, by popular imageries of criminality [1978: 565].

This popular imagery of criminality is often race specific. In a recent article, Liskia and Tausig (1979), reexamined 17 juvenile justice studies which considered the relationship between social class, race, and legal decision making. They observed strong race differences producing a cumulative racial effect transforming heterogenous prearrest populations into homogeneous institutional non-white populations. Thus, initial racial disparities are compounded at successive stages of the juvenile justice system. Finally, in a recent examination of the application of criminal labels, Bernstein et al. conclude:

Specifically, we interpret our findings to suggest that greater attention be paid to (1) organizational imperatives of the deviance controlling agency, (2) the expectations and values of those participating in the decisions and (3) the role of accumulated disadvantaged status acquired in prior deviance processing stages [1977: 754].

Organizational Characteristics and Criminal Processing

An accumulating body of research suggests that the ecology of criminal justice decision making or relevant organizational characteristics may have a direct impact on outcomes especially for non-white offenders. Hagan (1977), for example, examined the importance of urban and rural court settings and their impact for differential decisions affecting American Indians and whites. Direct race effects were found to exist in rural settings with American Indians receiving the more severe dispositions while racial effects were indirect in urban settings. Similarly, Austin (1980) found that the urban-rural factor accounted for substantial variation in the sentences imposed on convicted felony offenders. Austin notes that his findings support previous research in that

Suburban and especially rural as compared to urban courts sentenced both non-white and older offenders to prison in disproportionate numbers, notwithstanding the absence of relevant legal variables. It can tentatively be concluded that urban courts appear to adopt a more legalistic model of sentencing than either rural or suburban courts [1980:12].

Clearer support for an organizational hypothesis is seen in a recent study of decision making in the Massachusetts Division of Youth Services (Coates et al., 1978). As the authors note:

We have discovered a fairly classic example of organizational labeling. In this instance, the early detention decisions, which seem haphazard at best, serve to attach lasting labels to youth. These labels are regarded by persons in the corrections system as characteristic of youth and are relied upon as a basis for making placement and treatment decisions. Not only does the fact of detention adversely affect future decisions, but also the place where one is detained [1978: 62].

Their analysis indicates that neither delinquent history nor offense-related variables explains either that fact of detention or the place of detention. The most important explanatory factor in such decisions is the region of the state where the youth is processed. Thus, characteristics of the youth correctional system (e.g., availability of alternative detention facilities across the state) determine place of detention and not the characteristics of youth. Yet, for future decision makers those placed in secure custody facilities are somehow considered more dangerous, more "hard-core," more recidivistic than their counterparts housed elsewhere. This line of reasoning runs contrary to the actual data at hand. Cicourel (1968), Emerson (1979), Sprowls (1980), Eisenstein and Jacobs (1971), Figueira-McDonoug (1979), and others provide support for the role of organizational factors in criminal justice decision making.

In a recent examination of the processing of violent delinquents in three metropolitan New York counties, Strasburg (1978) discovered that official responses varied substantially depending upon the county in which the case was processed. This finding was coupled with racial differences in the processing of violent delinquents. As an aggregate figure, non-whites in all three counties were released at about half the rate of whites following adjudication. Further, in a recent examination of felony sentencing practices in the state of Michigan, Zallman et al. (1979) found significant and substantial differences in treatment of white and non-white offenders in that non-whites were treated more severly. These differences were found to vary depending upon the county in which the offender was processed. Brown (1979), in an examination of parole outcomes, found that Black inmates experienced inequities that were partially dependent upon the particular institution in which the inmate served his time. In summarizing much of the literature, Vold and Bernard conclude:

> All of these examples demonstrate that the official definition of individuals as criminal, as well as the official portrayal of criminal actions, is strongly affected by the organizational structure and policies of the criminal justice agencies, as well as by the personal characteristics of the criminal justice personnel. It is only by further study of the processes of social control that the relationship of officially defined crimes and criminals to the actual incidence of criminal behavior in society can be understood [1979: 273].

Hopefully, this brief overview of selected issues regarding race and crime has raised some questions and has indicated the necessity of continued research and knowledge gathering. Historically, theory and research are relatively weak in attempting to understand the relationship between race and crime although there has been marked improvement over the last few years. Continued methodological development, increased scrutiny of the criminal justice decision making process, and continued questioning are healthful signs. Racial issues cannot be ignored and public policy cannot be guided by ignorance. The catalyst of the recent riot in Miami was the acquittal by an all-white jury of four white police officers charged with the brutal fatal beating of a black man. This instance of collective violence was largely a response to perceived injustice on the part of the criminal justice system. If such injustices are not eliminated, continued dissatisfaction and violence will be assured with an ever-widening gap between majority and minority Americans.

Organization of the Book

This collection represents one attempt to deal with some of the many issues regarding the relationship between race, crime, and the criminal justice system. Each article represents a distinct contribution to this area and hopefully will be carefully scrutinized by the reader. While one may not agree with some of the points of view being offered, they will have served their purpose if they invite frank discussion and continued concern. Structurally, this book is divided into three sections. The first section provides two examples dealing with racial bias in the criminal justice system. McNeely and Pope examine the question of black overinvolvement in criminal activity while Bondavalli and Bondavalli review the "state of the art" regarding Hispanics and the criminal justice system. The second section includes four empirical articles examining the racial aspects of criminal justice decision making. Bynum utilizes path-analytic techniques to assess the relationship between parole outcome and race, specifically focusing on American Indians. Fyfe deals with the use of extreme force by New York City police officers against white and non-white suspects. Schuster's cohort study investigates possible differences between Black and white violent delinquents. Feyerherm, utilizing data from 10 California counties, examines the influence of extralegal factors on the disposition of status offenders. The final section of the book presents two possible models for change. The first, by Parnell, focuses upon the concept of community justice while the second, by Debro, examines the role of criminal justice education programs in Black colleges and universities. Each section is preceded by a summary of the major points.

REFERENCES

Austin, T. L. (forthcoming) "The influence of court location on type of criminal sentencing: The rural-urban factor." *Journal of Criminal Justice.*

Balbus, I. D. (1973) *The Dialectics of Legal Repression: Black Rebels Before the American Criminal Courts.* New York: Russell Sage Foundation.

Bensing, R. C. and O. Schroder (1960) *Homicide in an Urban Community.* Springfield, IL: Charles C Thomas.

Bernstein, I. N., W. R. Kelley, and P. A. Doyle (1977) "Societal reactions to deviants: The cost of criminal definitions." *American Sociological Review* (October): 1.

Brown, R. M. (1979) "Historical patterns of American violence" in H. D. Graham and T. R. Gurr (eds.) *Violence in America.* Beverly Hills, CA: Sage.

Brown, S. V. (1979) "Race and parole outcome hearings" in R. Alverez et al. (eds.) *Discrimination in Organizations.* San Francisco: Jossey-Bass.

Bullock, H. A. (1961) "Significance of the racial factor in the length of prison sentence." *Journal of Criminal Law, Criminology and Police Science* 52: 411-417.

Burke, P. and A. Turk (1975) "Factors affecting post-arrest dispositions: A model for analysis." *Social Problems* 22: 313-332.

Button, J. W. (1978) *Black Violence*. Princeton, NJ: Princeton University Press.
Cicourel, A. V. (1968) *The Social Organization of Juvenile Justice*. New York: Wiley.
Coates, R, A. D. Miller, and L. E. Ohlin (1978) *Diversity in a Youth Correctional System: Handling Delinquents in Massachusetts*. Cambridge, MA: Ballinger.
Cohen, L. E. and J. R. Kluegel (1979) "Selecting delinquents for adjudication: An analysis of intake screening decisions in two metropolitan juvenile courts." *Journal of Research in Crime and Delinquency* 16: 143-163.
––– (1978) "Determinants of juvenile court dispositions: Ascriptive and achieved factors in two metropolitan Courts." *American Sociological Review* (April): 162-176.
Cordner, G. T. Bynum, and J. Greene (1980) "The impacts of victim characteristics on police investigative decision-making." Presented at the annual meetings of the Midwest Sociological Society. Milwaukee, Wisconsin.
Curtis, L. A. (1975) *Violence, Race and Culture*. Lexington, MA: D.C. Heath.
Degher, D. W. (1975) "Native Americans in the justice system: An analysis of two rural Washington counties." Ph.D. dissertation, Washington State University.
Dison, J. E. (1976) "An empirical examination of conflict theory: Race and sentence length." Ph.D. dissertation, North Texas State University.
Eisenstein, J. and H. Jacobs (1971) *Felony Justice*. Boston: Little, Brown.
Emerson, R. M. (1969) *Judging Delinquents: Context and Process in the Juvenile Court*. Chicago: Aldine.
Farrell, R. A. and V. L. Swigert (1978) "Legal disposition of inter-group and intra-group homicides." *Sociological Quarterly* 19: 565-576.
Figueira-McDonough, J. (1979) "Processing juvenile delinquency in two cities: A cross-national comparison." *Journal of Research in Crime and Delinquence* 16: 114-144.
Foley, L. and C. E. Rasche (1979) "The effect of race on sentence, actual time served and final dispositions of female offenders" in J. A. Conley (ed.) *Theory and Research in Criminal Justice: Current Perspectives*. Cincinnati: Anderson.
Garfinkle, H. (1949) "Research note on inter- and intra-racial homicides." *Social Forces* 27: 369-381.
Gibson, J. (1978) "Race as a determinant of criminal sentences: A methodological critique and a case study." *Law and Society Review* 12: 455-478.
Green, E. (1964) "Inter- and intra-racial crime relative to sentencing." *Journal of Criminal Law, Criminology and Police Science* 55: 348-358.
––– (1961) *Judicial Attributes in Sentencing*. New York: Macmillan.
Grob, G. N. (1973) *Mental Institutions in America: Social Policy to 1875*. New York: Free Press.
Gurr, T. R. (1979) "Protest and rebellion in the 1960's" in H. D. Graham and T. R. Gurr (eds.) *Violence in America*. Beverly Hills, CA: Sage.
Hagan, J. (1977) "Criminal justice in rural and urban communities: A study of the bureaucratization of justice." *Social Forces* 55: 597-612.
––– (1974) "Extra-Legal attributes and criminal sentencing: An assessment of a sociological viewpoint." *Law and Society Review* 8: 357-383.
Hahn, H. and J. R. Feagin (1970) "Riot-precipitating police practices: Attitudes in urban ghettos." *Phylon* 31: 183-193.
Hall, E. L. and A. A. Simkus (1975) "Inequality in the types of sentences reviewed by Native Americans and whites." *Criminology* 13: 199-122.

Hepburn, J. R. (1978) "Race and the decision to arrest: An analysis of warrants issued." *Journal of Research in Crime and Delinquency* 15: 54-73.

Hindelang, M. J. (1975) *Opinion Regarding Crime, Criminal Justice and Related Topics* (SD-AR-1). Washington, DC: Government Printing Office.

——— (1969) "Equality under the law." *Journal of Criminal Law, Criminology and Police Science* 60: 306-313.

Holland, T. R. and N. S. Johnson (1979) "Offender ethnicity and presentence decision-making: A multivariate analysis." *Criminal Justice and Behavior* 6: 227-238.

Johnson, G. (1941) "The negro and crime." *American Academy of Political and Social Sciences* 271: 93-104.

Kritzer, H. M. (1977) "Political protest and political violence: A nonrecursive causal model." *Social Forces* 55: 630-640.

Liazos, A. (1972) "The poverty of the sociology of deviance: Nuts, sluts and preverts." *Social Problems* 20: 103-120.

Liska, A. E. and M. Tausig (1979) "Theoretical interpretations of social class and racial differentials in legal decision-making for juveniles." *Sociological Quarterly* 20: 197-207.

Lizotte, A. J. (1978) "Extra-legal factors in Chicago's criminal courts: Testing the conflict model of criminal justice." *Social Problems* 25: 564-580.

McNeely, R. L. and C. E. Pope (1978) "Race and involvement in common law personal crime: A response to Hindelang." *Review of Black Political Economy* 8: 405-410.

Moore, J. W. (1978) *Homeboys: Gangs, Drugs, and Prison in the Barrios of Los Angeles*. Philadelphia: Temple University Press.

Moore, L. A. and P. M. Roesti (1980) "Race and two juvenile justice system decision points: The filing of a petition and declaration of wardship." Presented at the annual meeting of the Midwest Sociological Association, Milwaukee, Wisconsin.

Meyers, M. A. (1979) "Official parties and official reactions: Victims and the sentencing of criminal defendants." *Sociological Quarterly* 20: 529-540.

——— and J. Hagan (1979) "Private and public trouble: Prosecutors and the allocation of court resources." *Social Problems* 26: 439-451.

National Council on the Aging (1975) *The Myth and Reality of Aging in America*. Washington, DC: Government Printing Office.

Parisi, N., M. R. Gottfredson, M. J. Hindelang, and T. J. Flanagan (1979) *Sourcebook of Criminal Justice Statistics–1978*. Washington, DC: Government Printing Office.

Platt, T. and P. Takagi (1977) "Intellectuals for law and order: A critique of the new realists." *Crime and Social Justice* 8 (Winter).

Pope, C. E. (1979) "Race and crime revisited." *Crime and Delinquency* (Summer): 347-357.

——— (1978) "Post arrest release decisions: An empirical examination of social and legal criteria." *Journal of Research in Crime and Delinquency* (January): 35-53.

——— (1976) "The influence of social and legal factors on sentence dispositions: A preliminary analysis of offender based transaction statistics." *Journal of Criminal Justice* 4: 203-221.

Radzinowicz, S. L. and J. King (1977) *The Growth of Crime*. New York: Basic Books.

Reasons, C. E. (1972) "Crime and the Native American" in C. E. Reasons and E. Kykendall (eds.) *Crime, Race and Justice*. Santa Monica, CA: Goodyear.

Silberman, C. E. (1978) *Criminal Violence, Criminal Justice*. New York: Random House.

Skogan, W. G. (1979) "Crime in contemporary America," in H. D. Graham and T. R. Gurr (eds.) *Violence in America*. Beverly Hills, CA: Sage.

Sprowls, J. T. (1980) *Discretion and Lawlessness: Compliance in the Juvenile Court*. Lexington, MA: Lexington.

Stewart, O. C. (1964) "Questions regarding American Indian criminality." *Human Organization* 23: 63-66.

Strasburg, P. A. (1978) *Violent Delinquents*. New York: Monarch.

Sutton, L. P. (1975) "Criminal sentencing: An empirical analysis of variations in sentences imposed in federal district courts." Ph.D. Dissertation, State University of New York at Albany.

Thio, A. (1973) "Class bias in the sociology of deviance." *American Sociologist* 8: 1-12.

Thomas, C. C. and R. J. Cage (1977) "The effect of social characteristics on juvenile court dispositions." *Sociological Quarterly* 18: 237-252.

Thornbery, T. P. (1973) "Race, socioeconomic status and sentencing in the juvenile justice system." *Journal of Criminal Law and Criminology* 64: 90-98.

Uhlman, T. M. (1979) *Racial Justice*. Lexington, MA: Lexington.

Unnever, J. D., C. E. Frazier, and J. C. Henretta (1980) "Race differences in criminal sentencing." *Sociological Quarterly* 21: 197-205.

Vines, K. and H. Jacob (1962) "Studies in judicial politics." *Tulane Studies in Political Science* 8.

Vold, G. B. and T. J. Bernard (1979) *Theoretical Criminology*. New York: Oxford University Press.

Wilson, J. Q. (1975) *Thinking About Crime* New York: Random House.

Woodson, R. T. [ed.] (1977) *Black Perspectives in Crime and the Criminal Justice System*. Boston: G. K. Hall.

Zallman, M., C. W. Ostrom, Jr., P. Guilliams, and G. Peaslee (1979) *Sentencing in Michigan* (Report of the Michigan Felony Sentencing Project). East Lansing: Michigan State Government.

Zingraff, M. T. and R. J. Thomson (1979) "Detecting sentencing disparity: Some problems and evidence." Presented at the annual meeting of the Society for the Study of Social Problems, Boston.

II.

Race-Related Problems and Criminal Justice:
Two Examples

Research examining race-related problems in crime and justice often focuses on discriminatory treatment in arrest, charging, conviction, and sentencing. Numerous studies, but not all, indicate that Blacks and members of other national minority-group populations are more likely to be arrested, charged, convicted, and receive longer sentences than whites for identical crimes. Studies rebutting these findings tend to emphasize that the actual involvement of Blacks and other minorities in crime is higher than that of the general population. McNeely and Pope argue that there is no definitive answer to the question of whether disproportionate minority incarceration rates are due to differential selection and other biases or to higher rates of minority involvement in crime.

They present two main themes. First, they stress the importance of socioeconomic factors in explaining race-related overinvolvement in crime for those who argue its existence, yet fail to take such factors into account. To illustrate the possible significance of socioeconomic status as it relates to criminal involvement, they select for particular attention the crime of rape because the potential influence of such factors is less clear for this offense, compared to many other crimes of violence. They stress that failure to underscore the role of socioeconomic factors when examining differences in criminal involvement by various racial groups may lead to suggestions that something inherent in racial status explains any differences. Second, they detail a variety of problems associated with gathering data on crime rates to buttress their contention that there is no definitive answer to the thesis of black overinvolvement. Simply put, traditional techniques for examining the characteristics of criminal offenders are not congruent measures of the same phenomena.

Bondavalli and Bondavalli draw attention to the special problems encountered by Spanish-speaking offenders emphasizing the significance of disparate cultural patterns and socioeconomic factors. Noting the rapid growth of the Spanish-speaking population in the United States, they point out that it is difficult to determine the extent of criminal involvement by individuals of Hispanic origin due to several problems, including the fact that such individuals are not uniformly designated as Spanish-speaking in official crime reports.

Limitations in the collection of data on Hispanics, the authors observe, have reduced the ability of researchers to examine issues concerning discriminatory treatment. However, they draw attention to the perceived mistreatment of Spanish-speaking persons, pointing out, among other problems, those of communication and underrepresentation of Hispanics in law enforcement roles. They also emphasize the need for interpreters whose presence in court might insure that defendants clearly comprehend the consequences of pleading guilty, waiving the right to counsel, or possibly more confusing procedures such as plea bargaining. Citing relevant court cases and literature, the authors also note that general cultural differences present the Spanish-speaking offenders with a host of problems that neither they nor the criminal justice system is currently capable of handling. Until major legal and policy changes are forthcoming, Spanish-speaking individuals will continue to be deprived of basic rights and liberties.

2

SOCIOECONOMIC AND RACIAL
ISSUES IN THE MEASUREMENT
OF CRIMINAL INVOLVEMENT

R. L. McNeely and Carl E. Pope
University of Wisconsin—Milwaukee

That Blacks in American society have been subjected, historically, to a variety of inequalities is well-known and requires no documentation here. However, arguments have been made recently that racial factors are of declining significance insofar as such factors relate to the treatment of Blacks in the economic realm (Wilson, 1978). Saliently, this point is made only with reference to specific subsets of the Black U.S. population (cf. Brimmer, 1973; Danziger and Lampman, 1978: 29-30). Although it is true that well-educated whites in recent years (cf. Featherman and Haueser, 1976; National Urban League, 1978: iv), it is not argued by proponents of the "declining significance of race" viewpoint that most Blacks are no longer exposed to historically rooted current forms of economic subordination (Wilson, 1978: 152). Given this subordination, and its possible relevance in explaining race-related criminal involvement, it is useful to briefly detail racial differences along selected socioeconomic lines.

SOCIOECONOMIC STATUS OF BLACK AMERICANS

The most recent relevant Bureau of Census data (July 1978) indicate that a full 31.3% of the Black population, compared to only 8.9% of the white population, is below the official "poverty line." These rates—computed for 1977, the year that Blacks experienced the highest numerical unemployment ever recorded since the government began compiling such statistics by race (National Urban League, 1978: iii)—represent a slight increase in the proportion of Blacks in impoverished status and a slight decrease in white impoverishment, compared to 1976 (cf. U.S. Bureau of the Census, 1977).

The "poverty line" is based upon the Department of Agriculture's 1961 Economic Food Plan adjusted each year to reflect changes in the Consumer Price Index. Budgets based on this plan provide for austere subsistence living (cf. Miller, 1965: 94; Miller and Roby, 1970: 5; MacDonald, 1972: 10) and assume that someone in the poverty-line household has certain sophisticated food-purchasing and preparation skills (The President's Commission on Income Maintenance, 1971: 4-8). Other estimates of the extent of poverty, based on the concept of minimum adequacy rather than minimum subsistence, have chronicled that in the years during and since the decade of the 1960s, between 40% and 55% of the Black population has been either poor or near poor (Miller and Roby, 1970: 30; Ornati, 1972: 27; Miller, 1972a; National Urban League, 1977: 4; U.S. Bureau of the Census, 1977: 24).

Although certain subgroups of the Black population have experienced recent socioeconomic progress, other subgroups have experienced dire retrogression. One subgroup experiencing retrogression is the behaviorally volatile 16-to-19-year age group. In 1950, nearly 70% of Black men in this age group were counted in the labor force, but less than 40% were so counted in 1975 (National Urban League, 1977: 34). Joblessness among Black female teen-agers is even higher than it is among Black male teen-agers (National Urban League, 1978: 24). The official unemployment rate for Blacks in this age group is slightly less than 40% and the National Urban League estimates that the true rate (counting discouraged workers) of their unemployment has hovered recently between 60% (1978: 21) and 64% (1977: 34).

Not only has the ratio of earnings of the overall Black population relative to whites not changed appreciably since World War II (Miller, 1972b: 63), it has actually been declining in recent years. For example, in 1976 and 1977 the ratio of median Black to median white family income dropped to about 59% (computed from data compiled by the U.S. Bureau of the Census, 1977:7; 1978:7) from its previous high of 61% reached during 1969 and 1970 (U.S. Bureau of the Census, 1975: 25). These points are put into additional perspective when one considers that Black families with both spouses employed continue to earn only about 98% of what the white husband earns by himself (McNeely et al. 1979: 2). Finally, as official unemployment among whites dropped from 7% to 6.5% between 1976 and 1977, the official Black unemployment rate in 1977 stayed at 13.2% (National Urban League, 1978: iii). Estimates of the true (counting discouraged workers) 1977 unemployment rate for Blacks indicate that joblessness among these workers, for the third consecutive year, was really about 25% (National Urban League, 1978: 21). Thus, one out of every four Black workers was unemployed in 1975, 1976, and 1977.

These figures present a graphic picture of the experiential dissimilarities confronting Black versus white Americans. Significantly, this experiential dissimilarity has been found to be due principally to race, as opposed to other poverty-related factors. Research findings reported by Thernstrom (1969: 178-179), Duncan (1969), and Ornati (1972) indicate that when such factors as education, family background, family size, geographical location, and other variables are controlled, Blacks still do not earn nearly as much as whites. Siegel (1965) and Weiss (1970) have found that Blacks receive lower income returns to education than whites and, more recently, Wright (1978) has found similar results although discrepant earnings between Blacks and whites are explained in terms of the subjugation of racial groups into specified class categories.

Given the existence of race-related differences in the experiential realities confronting various racial groups, it is illogical to assume that inequalities in experiences will produce equalities of outcome. Insofar as this statement relates to Black overrepresentation in particular kinds of criminal categories, for example, excluding white-collar "upper-world" categories, one logically might expect some race-related overrepresentation because impoverishment is a virtual sine qua non for certain kinds of prestige-seeking or survival-related involvements in illegal activities (cf. Cloward and Ohlin, 1960; Swan, 1981.)

Although the reasons underlying possible disproportional involvement in some forms of criminal activity are, or should be, obvious, conceptualizing the possible influence of socioeconomic factors in the presumed overrepresentation by Blacks in other forms is not equally simple. For example, Hindelang (1978) has found recently that victim survey data show Blacks to be overrepresented compared to their population base in the common law personal crimes of robbery, assault, and rape. Of these three categories, the influence of socioeconomic factors in explaining possible overrepresentation probably is least clear for rape. For this reason, a brief discussion follows focusing upon how socioeconomic and selected cultural factors may converge to explain the possibility of racial overrepresentation. Remarks on this point are limited to the possible influence of these factors and it should be understood that the influence of the other factors (cf. Davis, 1976) is not taken into account. Specifically, within the context of the brief remarks on rape that follow, the objective is simply to direct attention to the importance of socioeconomic inequalities as they may relate to the Black overrepresentation presumption. Second, although the following remarks are focused on Blacks, much of what is said possibly may be generalized to members of other national minority groups who are victimized by social and economic inequalities.

SOCIOECONOMIC STATUS, RACE, AND RAPE

The precipitating role of assailants' feelings of personal victimization due to economic and other forms of subjugation resulting from the impact of extant patterns of racial discrimination has been well-known since 1968 (cf. Cleaver, 1968; Bacon, 1971: 22). As Eldridge Cleaver poignantly remarked when awakening to the implications of being Black in white America, "I was soon aflame with indignation over my newly discovered social status, and inwardly I turned away from America with horror, disgust and outrage. I did this consciously, deliberately, willfully, methodically . . . Rape was an insurrectionary act" (Cleaver, 1968: 4, 14).

The extent to which such feelings characterize Black male rapists is unknown although it is known that Black rapists tend to be from the lower socioeconomic classes (cf. Curtis, 1974). Although data obtained in some studies with largely Black sample populations suggest chance, situational factors, and material gain as the assailants' self-reported reasons for involvement (Landau, 1977), it has been noted that Black rapists, often very embittered about race-related social conditions, seek rape as a means of personal recourse yet are reluctant to discuss these feelings with white officials (Cleaver, 1968: 17). On this point Comer (1970) noted and Curtis (1975) later underscored the role of generalized feelings of social and economic victimization, particularly as experienced by young Black males, as precursors to assaultive behavior against whites. Curtis, discussing poor street corner males, remarked:

> A cognizance permeates to the ghetto's depths, especially among the young . . . it is logical to expect that interracial homicide and assault is a natural way of expressing nascent black power and identity among certain frustrated young black males who may already share contracultural values and behavior. These conjectures can be applied straightforwardly to rape [1976: 128].

These brief remarks strongly implicate the influence of race-related socioeconomic inequality in the occurence of interracial rape. Further, Curtis's focus on poor street cornor males and the fact that rapists tend to be of low socioeconomic status emphasize the significance of high unemployment among Blacks during their behaviorally volatile teen-age years, as well as of high Black unemployment in general.

The influence of various socioeconomic factors also may be seen in intraracial rape, which is reported more often and assumed to be more common. Curtis (1976) has developed a framework that focuses on the convergence of impoverishment, racism, and contracultural and subcultural factors to elucidate the phenomenon of Black involvement in rape, particularly Black-on-Black rape. In essence, Curtis specifies that Black males are likely to have these factors converge in ways that produce a high potential for involvement in sexually exploitive relationships with women, including forcible rape.

The basic thesis of Curtis's framework is that inadequate opportunities to secure gainful employment result in adaptations among poor Black males that stress the importance of physical toughness and sexual exploitation as a basis for developing the self-esteem (cf. Rainwater, 1970) that is largely denied them through conventional avenues. Specifically:

> Institutional racism blocks opportunities in the mode specified by Cloward and Ohlin (1960), creating economic marginality among blacks and inducing adaptations that include behaviors labeled discordant by those holding power and institutionalizing the racism. The argument, then, is that racial-economic constraints have causal primacy in determining black behavior . . . with only a limited

number of avenues open . . . a more distinguishable cluster highlighted by physical toughness and sexual exploitation emerges
among some poor black males than among middle-class black or
white males. The credibility of the process heightens when the
quality of youth is added to blackness, maleness, and poverty
[Curtis, 1976: 121, 122].

Another factor deemed important by Curtis, resulting chiefly and given
form principally by blocked economic opportunities and institutional
racism (Curtis, 1976; cf. McNeely, 1979: 14; Yinger, 1960), is what is
described as the Black contracultural pattern of greater acceptance and
justification of violence. Although it has been suggested that violence may
be accepted and justified more often by members of lower class groups,
Curtis points out that adherence to this pattern is intensified among Blacks
due to their unique experiences of southern slavery and violence and their
present-day racial victimization.

In sum, Curtis suggests that constrained opportunities and high unemployment combined with a greater acceptance of violence and status
seeking, based upon physical toughness and sexual exploitation, make
rejections for some, "harder to sustain and rationalize to self and others in
an inner-city setting that promotes male sexual prowess" (Curtis, 1976:
126). On this point it should be noted that 25% of Black-on-Black rape
victims have been found to be neighbors or close friends, and nearly 60%
knew their assailants prior to the assault (Amir, 1967: 70).

This discussion has stressed the importance of socioeconomic inequities
as they relate to the rape involvements of Black assailants. (Obviously,
similar lines of argument can be generalized to selected other criminal
offense categories.) In so doing, the argument is made that any possible
overrepresentation of Blacks in this criminal category is due to factors
apart from those inherent in racial status. This point is an extremely
important one to make by those subscribing to the racial overrepresentation hypothesis. Failure to do so underscores, by default, the long-
perpetuated impression that something inherent in racial status explains
any overinvolvement (cf. Wolfgang and Cohen, 1970: 10).

Although the role of socioeconomic status as it may relate to racial
disproportionality in criminal involvement has been emphasized, a number
of problems which make it impossible to answer definitively the question
of whether such disproportionality exists in fact have not been identified.
Hindelang's (1978) recent article strongly suggests that such dispropor-

tionality does exist. This contention is based upon recently collected victimization data that tend to support official crime estimates indicating the existence of racial disproportionality in criminal involvement. One significant problem associated with collecting victimization survey data is that one must rely on perceptions of victims which may or may not be accurate. The degree to which respondents accurately remember events within a given reference period and recount them factually is unclear. In detailing this and other problems associated with the measurement of criminal involvement, attention is directed away from the assailant in order to focus on victims and their perceptions.

VICTIMS, VICTIMIZATION SURVEYS, AND DISCREPANT PERCEPTION

There is no definitive body of knowledge concerning the accuracy of victims' perception regarding the characteristics of incidents and/or offenders. Allport and Postman's research reporting that white and Black subjects are very likely to perceive, remember, and interpret situations in quite opposite ways raises questions regarding the validity of perceptions of respondents across racial lines. They showed to Black and white subjects pictures that contain a white man holding a razor while arguing with a Black man. White subjects to whom these pictures were described by others tend to recall the Black as brandishing the razor (Allport and Postman, 1965: 56).

In another study, Secord et al. (1956) displayed pictures of 15 adult faces to white subjects whose attitudes about Blacks were known. Ten of the faces were of Blacks with widely varied physiognomic features. The other faces in the five remaining pictures were of whites. Subjects were asked to rate these pictures according to a number of characteristics. Once subjects characterized faces as those of Blacks, they proceeded to ascribe behaviors that were consistent with their stereotypical conceptions of Blacks, often paying no further attention whatsoever to differences among the individual faces portrayed in the pictures. These findings were consistent for the less prejudiced subjects as well as those more strongly prejudiced against Blacks.

The physical attractiveness of victims and assailants reportedly is related to sentence lengths recommended by jurors (Landy and Aronson,

1969) and positive or negative characteristics ascribed to rape defendants by jurors are related to racial similarities/disimilarities between jurors and defendants (Ugwuegbu, 1976). Miller and Hewitt have suggested that because "one of the strongest determinations of attractiveness is racial similarity, it would seem reasonable to speculate that a jury would be more likely to convict a defendant accused of rape when the victim and jurors were similar rather than dissimilar on the dimension of race" (1978: 159). They examined this proposition by showing subjects a videotape depicting the onset of an actual rape case involving a Black male defendant. Written summaries of prosecution and defense arguments used during the trial were provided each subject. Half of the subjects were informed that the victim was white and the other half were informed she was Black. Both Black and white simulated jurors were significantly more likely to vote for conviction when there was juror/victim similarity (Miller and Hewitt, 1978: 160).

Mayas (1977: 9) cites a study reporting similar results in which white children aged 8 to 10 were asked to select from a biracial set of photographs those individuals they believed to be murderers. Findings indicated a strong bias toward perceived Black male violence—Black males were perceived primarily as murderers and white males were not. Mayas suggests that these findings support the existence of "cognitive schemas" the predispose individuals to attribute criminality based on race-related stereotypes rather than on observable truth. Cognitive schemas are subjective networks that integrate information so that choices can be made in situations of relative ambiguity (Mayas, 1977:4).

The findings of these studies suggest that whites may characterize certain behaviors differently depending upon their perception of the racial identity of the antagonist. A belligerent attempt to establish contact with a white female stranger may be interpreted as an attempted rape if the person attempting to make contact is Black and it may be interpreted quite differently if he is not. Abbott and Calonico's (1974) study tends to underscore this assertion. They found that not only did newspaper accounts of rape overemphasize Black-on-white rape but also that white sample respondents perceived the reality of Black men raping white women as being consistent with the biased newspaper accounts versus actual rape statistics.

Goode (1969), discussing nonstranger rape, notes that discrepant perceptions occurring in lower class dating relationships can result in charges of rape or attempted rape. Although he does not specify Blacks, Goode points out that females, resisting sexual advances, may more often be perceived by lower class males as simply trying to create or maintain an image of respectability through feigned resistance. At the same time, the female expects that her trust in the male will not be violated and her resistance honored.

On these points overall, it has not been unknown for white women to mistakenly or intentionally identify innocent Blacks as rape assailants, and it has not been unknown for white rapists to use cosmetic applications that make them appear to their victims to be Black (Ginzberg, 1969).

The fact of differential perception across racial lines is particularly germane to crime categories other than rape where there is more likely to be interracial involvement. These categories include violent crimes such as homicide, robbery, and assault (Mayas, 1977). Mayas found that whites overwhelmingly (1) ascribe crimes of violence to Black perpetrators, even though insufficient evidence exists for such ascription; (2) ascribe nonviolent crimes overwhelmingly to whites, even though insufficient evidence exists for such ascription; (3) make substantially greater Black criminal attributions than do Blacks; (4) are less certain of their judgments than Blacks; and (5) judge identical crimes as far more serious if committed by Blacks than whites (Mayas, 1977). Such perceptual problems can distort findings based on victimization surveys in ways that are unknown and undefined.

At the same time, culture, socioeconomic status, and other factors may be converging in ways that produce actual disproportionalities of involvement. For example, homicide rates are much higher among lower class individuals and, therefore, among Blacks who are disproportionately lower class. Yet, consider the fact that, although their suicide rate over the last decade has been growing (Blocker, 1975; Slater, 1973), Blacks have significantly lower suicide rates than whites (Parker, 1974). Personal attributes and other factors associated with suicide are found much more prevalently among middle-class as opposed to lower class individuals (Bagley, 1973), possibly explaining the higher rate among whites (Henry and Short, 1965: 69-71). Interestingly, White (1975) found that when racial suicide and homicide rates are combined, at least for specified time periods and geographical locations, the proportion of actual fatalities for both groups is nearly equivalent. Again, the possible significance of socioeconomic and other converging factors is underscored.

Although we argue that racial overinvolvement, presuming its existence, is related to socioeconomic factors, it is important to reestablish the fact that presently there is no definitive answer to the overinvolvement question. For example, although victim survey results show non-whites to be overrepresented in common law personal crime, there are substantive methodological problems which question the validity of such findings. Recall and honesty of reporting are of primary concern. While reverse record checks—examination of police files for known victims—have been used to estimate the reliability of recall, little is known regarding the recall of those respondents who do not report incidents to the police. Further, reverse record checks have shown that victims tend not to recall those assaults and rapes in which the offender is related to the victim. Aside from faulty recall, there are additional factors that may contribute to distortions in reporting. Some victims may feel stigmatized by having been involved in the incident (especially in the case of rape) and not report it to the interviewer. Others may contribute a "reactive" effect by providing erroneous information to feel important or otherwise attempt to please the interviewer. An unknown proportion of respondents may report being the victim of a crime when, in fact, no criminal activity took place. Similarly, other respondents may not realize that they have been the victim of a crime. Such distortions, whether intentional or not, are likely to bias victim survey results.

The extent to which victim survey findings are comparable to other indices of crime is, at best, questionable. Victim survey techniques deal only with so called street crime while ignoring clandestine and "upper world" criminal activity. Embezzlement, price fixing, and similar "white collar" crimes are not tapped by these surveys. Victimization findings regarding disproportionate criminal involvement are strictly limited to accounts regarding offender characteristics derived from crimes of personal nature. Moreover, events reported by individuals must be recast into legally defined criminal acts in order to be congruent with official statistics regarding crime and delinquency. In a recent empirical attempt to compare victim and official statistics, Nelson (1978) found that correlations between the two sources for personal crime without theft (rape and aggravated and simple assault) were either negative or close to zero. This suggests that, for those personal crimes, victim and official tallies are measuring different phenomena.

Overall, victimization surveys suffer from severe biasing effects which make direct comparisons with other indices difficult if not impossible. Further, these biases are free to vary in unknown ways across different sampling frames and crime categories. As Hindelang and his colleagues note:

The technique of victimization surveying is only about a decade old. Although careful methodological work designed to improve the technique has been undertaken by LEAA and the Bureau of Census, it is erroneous and naive to believe that victimization survey results tell us what the "true" crime rate is. Just as traditional police statistics on offenses have known shortcomings that limit their utility, so do victimization surveys [1978: 227].

OFFICIAL STATISTICS *Notes*

Historically, data sources supporting the overrepresentation argument have focused upon official agency statistics in one form or another. For example, aggregate data regarding offenses known to the police and crimes cleared by arrest have been reported since the 1930s with the establishment of the Uniform Crime Reports (UCR). Similarly, national prisoner statistics focusing upon inmates institutionalized under state authority have been available for many years. Periodically, the Census Bureau has reported data relevant to criminal justice such as counts of prisoner populations. While these sources have often been criticized for their many inadequacies and shortcomings, they have frequently been used as a basis for exploring the relationship between race and crime.

Most introductory criminology texts at some point introduce UCR data showing a disproportionate arrest rate for Blacks and other minority groups. For example, Sutherland and Cressey (1970) present aggregate data from the 1969 UCR on the relationship between arrest offenses and race for the year 1968. These data show that, despite variations by specific offenses, Blacks are overrepresented in arrest figures with respect to their population base. The UCR data reported by Sutherland and Cressey, as well as that reported elsewhere (Mulvihill and Tumin, 1969), show that Black/white arrest differentials are far greater for crimes of violence than for property offenses. Other studies relying on a variety of official data sources have reached similar conclusions regarding Black overrepresentation. In examining the imprisonization rate for Blacks and whites, Bonger concluded:

These figures leave no room for doubt; crime among Negroes is significantly higher than among whites. It is three or four times higher among the men, and four or fives times higher among the women. To me this appears to eliminate the idea that actual criminality among Negroes is no greater than among whites [1969: 43].

Those findings based upon official data sources, however, do leave room for doubt. Often, those official statistics compiled by various government agencies prove to be unreliable, fragmentary, and misleading. For example, police jurisdictions serving only 77% of the U.S. population forward arrest data to the Federal Bureau of Investigation for inclusion in the uniform crime-reporting system. Data regarding felons institutionalized under state authority are based upon incomplete and inconsistent reporting. Other substantive problems focus upon the categorization of offenses, computation of base rates, weighting of seriousness, and the like (Doleschal and Wilkins, 1972; Hindelang, 1974). Further, the degree to which one can infer from arrest, conviction, and prison data to general rates of criminality is uncertain. The disproportionate arrest rate for Blacks may be the result of selection bias. Thus Blacks may be more likely than whites to be arrested, charged, and convicted while their crime rate in the general population may be similar to that of whites.

SELF-REPORT SURVEYS

Evidence supporting the above premise has frequently been found in the results obtained by self-report researchers. When respondents are asked to disclose (either by checklist or interview) their own previous criminal involvement, few racial differences are noted. That is, the distribution of self-reported criminal involvement for white and Black respondents is either zero or considerably less than that found in official statistics. In a quite detailed and comprehensive analysis of delinquent behavior, Hirschi (1969) utilized school records, self-report questionnaires, and official police data on 4,077 students from 11 public junior and senior high schools. Examining the distribution of delinquency within his sampling frame, Hirschi observed that

> Forty-two percent of the Negro and eighteen percent of the white boys in the analyzed sample had police records two years prior to adminstration of the questionnaire. When other measures of "delinquency" are used, the difference between Negros and whites is sharply reduced [1969: 75].

While there was a slight relationship between race and crime when measured by self-report responses (a difference of approximately five percentage points), official statistics substantially overestimated the magnitude of this relationship. Other self-report surveys examining the relationship between race and crime have found differences between Blacks and whites to be slight or non-existent (Pope, 1979).

Self-report surveys, however, suffer from some of the same methodological problems associated with victimization surveys. Questions concerning recall, honesty, and comparability of findings also plague self-report researchers. Again, the question arises as to whether respondents can accurately recall and honestly report events occurring within a stipulated time frame. Such concerns are especially acute considering the fact that most self-report research has focused on samples of juveniles within high school populations. Further, self-report findings are not directly comparable to official statistics since these findings are generally weighted toward trivial incidents (Hood and Sparks, 1970; Nettler, 1978). For example, many of those items frequently included in self-report checklists focus on the incidence and prevalence of smoking cigarettes, consuming alcoholic beverages, disobeying one's parents, and similar activities. These events are not major criminal activities and may, in fact, reflect normal experiences in growth and development. It should also be noted that relatively few self-report studies have examined racial differences among respondents and that the sample of Black respondents utilized in most self-report research has been relatively small. Finally, self-report research primarily focuses upon a respondent's perception of past activity—perception that may be distorted across divergent samples and in unknown ways.

CONCLUSION

This article has examined the measurement of crime as it relates to differential involvement of Blacks and whites in some detail. Recent victimization findings have shown that Blacks are overrepresented with regard to their population base in common law personal crimes of rape, robbery, and assault. These findings are supportive of official statistics which have traditionally shown Blacks and other minority groups to be differentially involved in criminal events. Self-report surveys, on the other hand, have reached opposite conclusions. When asked to self-disclose their own criminal involvement, Black and white respondents reveal either zero or minimal differences. Some have attempted to argue that victim surveys resolve the discrepancy between official and self-report measures and thus the disproportionate involvement is indeed a true relationship. Such conclusions are, at best premature.

Each measurement source suffers from distinct methodological biases which render any conclusions regarding race and crime questionable. Similarly, any attempt to examine the relationship between race and crime must take into account the historical and contemporary disadvantaged status of Blacks and other minorities compared to that of whites. The issues raised in this article must be carefully considered in order that future research dealing with race and crime does not unintentionally become part of the bibliographic arsenal of the forces arguing in favor of retrenchment and racial repression in this country.

REFERENCES

Abbott, D. and J. Calonico (1974) "Black man, white woman – the maintenance of a myth: Rape and the press in New Orleans." In M. Riedel and T. Thornberry (eds.) *Crime and Delinquency: Dimensions of Deviance.* New York: Praeger.

Allport, G. and L. Postman (1965) "The basic psychology of rumor." Pp. 47-58 in E. Proshansky and B. Seidenberg (eds.) *Basic Studies in Social Psychology.* New York: Holt, Rinehart and Winston.

Amir, M. (1967) "Patterns in forcible rape." Pp. 93-102 in M. Clinard and R. Quinney (eds.) *Criminal Behavior Systems: A Typology.* New York: Holt, Rinehart and Winston.

Bacon, D. (1977) "Young blacks out of work: Time bomb for U.S." *U.S. News and World Report* (December 5): 22-25.

Bagley, C. (1973) "Occupational class and symptoms of depression." *Social Science and Medicine* 7: 327-340.

Blocker, U. (1975) "Black suicide: An exploratory study." *Smith College Studies in Social Work* 46(1): 26.

Bonger, W. A. [Margaret Mathews Hordyk, tr.] (1969) *Race and Crime.* (1940: reprinted.) Montclair, NJ: Patterson Smith.

Brimmer, A. F. (1973) "Employment and income in the black community: Trends and outlook." Los Angeles: University California Committee on Public Lectures, Institute of Government and Public Affairs.

Cleaver, E. (1968) *Soul on Ice.* New York: McGraw-Hill.

Cloward, R. and L. E. Ohlin (1960) *Delinquency and Opportunity.* New York: Free Press.

Comer, J. P. (1970) "The dynamics of black and white violence." Pp. 444-464 in H. D. Graham and T. R. Gurr (eds.) *Violence in America: Historical and Comparative Perspectives.* (A Report Submitted to the National Commission on the Causes and Preventions of Violence.) New York: Bantam.

Curtis, L. (1976) "Rape, race, and culture: Some speculations in search of a theory." Pp. 117-134 in M. J. Walker and S. L. Brodsky (eds.) *Sexual Assault*. Lexington, MA: Lexington.

——— (1975) *Violence, Rape, and Culture*. Lexington, MA: Lexington.

——— (1974) *Criminal Violence: National Patterns and Behavior*. Lexington, MA: Lexington.

Davis, J. A. (1976) "Blacks, crime, and American culture." *Annals of the American Academy of Political and Social Science* 423 (January): 89-98.

Doleschal, E. and L. T. Wilkins (1972) *Criminal Statistics*. Washington, DC: Government Printing Office.

Duncan, O. (1969) "Inheritance of poverty or inheritance of race." Pp. 85-110 in D. Moynihan (ed.) *On Understanding Poverty*. New York: Basic Books.

Featherman, D. and R. M. Haveser (1976) "Changes in the socioeconomic stratification of the races." *American Journal of Sociology* 82: 621-655.

Ginzburg, R. [ed.] (1969) *One Hundred Years of Lynchings*. New York: Lancer.

Goode, W. J. (1969) "Violence between intimates." Pp. 941-979 in D. J. Mulvihill et al. (eds.) *Crimes of Violence*. Washington, DC: Government Printing Office.

Hindelang, M. J. (1978) "Race and involvement in common law personal crimes." *American Sociological Review* 43: 93-109.

——— (1974) "The uniform crime report revisited." *Journal of Criminal Justice* 2: 1-18.

——— M. R. Gottfredson and J. Garofalo (1978) *Victims of Personal Crime: An Empirical Formulation for a Theory of Personal Victimization*. Cambridge, MA: Ballinger.

Hirschi, T. (1969) *Causes of Delinquency*. Berkeley: University of California Press.

Hood, R. and R. Sparks (1970) *Key Issues in Criminology*. New York: McGraw-Hill.

Landau, S. (1976) "The sex offender's perception of his victim: Some cross-cultural findings." Presented at the Second International Symposium on Victimology, Boston.

Landy, D. and E. Aronson (1969) "The influence of the character of the criminal and his victim on the decisions of simulated jurors." *Journal of Experimental Social Psychology* 5: 141-152.

MacDonald, D. (1972) "Our invisible poor." Pp. 7-24 in L. A. Ferman et al. (eds.) *Poverty in America*. Ann Arbor: University of Michigan Press.

Mayas, J. (1977) "Perceived criminality: The attribution of criminal race from news-reported crime." Ph.D. dissertation, University of Michigan.

McNeely, R. L. (1979) "Sources of alienation at work and household violence." *Journal of Social Development Issues* 3 (Spring): 12-34.

——— J. M. Jones, and R. L. Impink (1979) "Labor force involvement of Milwaukee's working women." University of Wisconsin—Milwaukee Urban Observatory.

Miller, H. (1972a) "Poverty and the Negro." Pp. 160-176 in L. A. Ferman et al. (eds.) *Poverty in America*. Ann Arbor: University of Michigan Press.

——— (1972b) "Is the income gap closed?" "No!" Pp. 61-66 in L. A. Ferman et al. (eds.) *Poverty in America*. Ann Arbor: University of Michigan Press.

——— (1965) "Changes in the number and composition of the poor." Pp. 81-101 in M. S. Gordon (ed.) *Poverty in America*. San Francisco: Chandler.

Miller, M. and J. Hewitt (1978) "Conviction of a defendant as a function of juror-victim racial similarity." *Journal of Social Psychology* 105: 159-160.

Miller, S. M. and P. Roby (1970) *The Future of Inequality*. New York: Basic Books.

Mulvihill, D. J. and M. M. Tumin (1969) *Crimes of Violence*. (A Staff Report Submitted to the National Commission on the Causes and Prevention of Violence.) Washington, DC: Government Printing Office.

National Urban League (1978) *The State of Black America 1978*. New York: Author.

——— (1977) *The State of Black America 1977*. New York: Author.

Nelson, J. F. (1978) "Alternative measures of crime: A comparison of the Uniform Crime Report and the National Crime Survey in 26 American cities." Presented at the annual meeting of the American Society of Criminology.

Nettler, G. (1978) *Explaining Crime*. New York: McGraw-Hill.

Ornati, O. (1972) "Poverty in America." Pp. 24-39 in L. A. Ferman et al. (eds.) *Poverty in America*. Ann Arbor: University of Michigan Press.

Parker, A. (1974) *Suicide Among Young Adults*. New York: Exposition Press.

Pope, C. E. (1979) "Race and crime revisited." *Crime and Delinquency* 25: 347-357.

The President's Commission on Income Maintenance (1971) "Poverty in America: Dimensions and prospects." Pp. 3-27 in T. Marmour (ed.) *Poverty Policy*. Chicago: Aldine-Atherton.

Rainwater, L. (1970) *Behind Ghetto Walls: Black Families in a Federal Slum*. Chicago: Aldine.

Secord, P. F., W. Beven, and B. Katz (1956) "Perceptual accentuation and the Negro stereotype." *Journal of Abnormal Social Psychology* 53: 78-83.

Siegel, P. (1965) "On the costs of being a Negro." *Sociological Inquiry* 35 (Winter): 41-57.

Slater, J. (1973) "Suicide: A growing meance." *Ebony* (September): 156-165.

Sutherland, E. H. and D. R. Cressey (1970) *Criminology*. Philadelphia: Lippincott.

Swan, L. A. (forthcoming) "Criminal behavior and the reentry of formerly incarcerated black men into society." Chapter 6 in L. A. Swan, *Survival and Progress: The Afro-American Experience*. Westport, CT: Greenwood.

Thernstrom, S. (1969) "Poverty in historical perspective." Pp. 160-186 in D. Moynihan (ed.) *On Understanding Poverty*. New York: Basic Books.

Ugwuegbu, D.C.E. (1976), "Black juror's personality trial attribution to a rape case defendant." *Social Behavior and Personality* 4: 193-201.

U.S. Bureau of The Census (1978) "Money income in 1977 of households in the United States." *Current Population Reports*, Series P-60, No. 117. Washington, DC: Government Printing Office.

——— (1977) "Money income and poverty status of families and persons in the United States: 1976." *Current Population Reports*, Series P-60, No. 107. Washington, DC: Government Printing Office.

——— (1975) "The social and economic status of the black population in the United States:: 1974." *Current Population Reports*, Series P-23, No. 54. Washington, DC: Government Printing Ofice.

Weiss, R. (1970) "The effects of education on the earnings of blacks and whites." *Review of Economics and Statistics* 52: 150-159.

White, J. (1975) "A comparative analysis of black homicide and white suicide among youth." Heller School for Advanced Studies in Social Welfare, Brandeis University.

Wilson, W. J. (1978) *The Declining Significance of Race.* Chicago: University of Chicago Press.

Wolfgang, M. E. and B. Cohen (1970) *Crime and Race.* New York: Institute of Human Relations Press.

Wright, E. (1978) "Race, class, and income equality." *American Journal of Sociology* 83: 1368-1397.

Yinger, M. (1960) "Contraculture and subculture." *American Sociological Review* 25: 625-635.

3

SPANISH-SPEAKING PEOPLE AND THE NORTH AMERICAN CRIMINAL JUSTICE SYSTEM

Bonnie J. Bondavalli

Illinois State University

Bruno Bondavalli

University of Illinois

INTRODUCTION

The number of Spanish-speaking persons residing in the United States is growning rapidly. Spanish-origin individuals numbered approximately 9.1 million according to the 1970 census, accounting for 4.4% of the total population (U.S. Department of Commerce, *Subject Reports*, 1973). Spanish was the second most common mother tongue of those included in the census (U.S. Department of Commerce, *Detailed Characteristics*, 1973). These figures probably underestimate the number of Hispanics in the United States. The Census Bureau has had difficulty conceptually defining the Hispanic population, for example, Spanish language, Spanish heritage, Spanish surname, or self-identification as Hispanic (U.S. Commission on Civil Rights, 1974; Hernandez et al., 1973). Moreover, a considerable number of individuals fitting the census definitions may not have been counted as the census is believed to have ignored large numbers of urban poor. Also not included were an estimated 7.4 million illegal aliens. The 1978 census estimates approximately 12 million Hispanic Americans, but many continue to believe that Spanish-origin individuals are seriously undercounted and that the total number is closer to 19 million (It's Your Turn in the Sun," 1978).

Whatever the exact number of Spanish-heritage residents in the United States, the figure is large and is increasing at a dramatic pace. The issue of crime in the Spanish-speaking community is just beginning to receive the attention it warrants. Given the characteristics of many of the Spanish-speaking individuals, it would appear that they constitute a "population at risk" in terms of crime. According to the census reports, while the median age of the total U.S. population is 28.5, the median age of persons of Puerto Rican origin is 19.8; and the median age of those of Mexican origin is 18.9. The median income of Spanish-origin men with incomes is about $2,000 less than the median income of all men with incomes. The unemployment rate among Spanish-speaking persons is higher than the unemployment rate for the total population by 2.8%. About 1 in 5 Spanish-speaking adults (compared to 1 in 20 men and 1 in 25 women in the nation as a whole) has completed less than five years of school; and 83% of the Spanish-speaking families in the United States live in metropolitan areas (U.S. Department of Commerce, 1975). Although more recent reports show that the incomes and educational levels of Hispanics are rising, they remain low relative to most other groups (U.S. Commission on Civil Rights, *Social Indicators*, 1978).

Further, some researchers have noted emotional as well as socio-economic factors which could conceivably contribute to crime in the Spanish-speaking community. Henggler and Tavormina's study of children of Mexican-American migrant workers, for example, indicated that the children showed a pattern of vulnerability on emotional, as well as verbal weaknesses on intellectual, indices (1978: 103-104). Indeed, living and working in an alien society can itself involve "a profound challenge . . . to one's problem-solving abilities and to one's ability to maintain emotional composure" (Guthrie, 1975: 96).

DETERMINING THE SCOPE OF THE PROBLEM

Arrest Reports

At present, it is difficult to assess the extent of the crime problem among Spanish-speaking individuals. The Federal Bureau of Investigation which assembles the Uniform Crime Reports does not at present distinguish Hispanic persons in their arrest data. If state crime-reporting agencies choose to gather such information, they can, but it appears that few do. (Table 1 shows the type of information which can be assembled from the Illinois crime reports.)

Among the few states which collect relevant data, definitions of the relevant population and reporting practices vary. In Illinois, for example, "Mexican" and "Puerto Rican" are listed as racial categories; but each police department is left to determine who should be placed in these categories (Towner, 1978). Also, reporting procedures in Chicago reduce the validity of the data still further (Statistical Analysis Center, N.D.: 34-42).

Court Statistics

Relevant court statistics are even more difficult to locate. Several years ago, the Law Enforcement Assistance Administration (LEAA) began providing funds for the development of a computerized information system for the courts. The Prosecution Management Information System (PROMIS) is now in differing stages of development in the various jurisdictions. It permits classification of clients by race and, if desired, by ethnicity. Only Los Angeles County, San Diego County, Tallahassee, and Manhattan list Hispanic ethnicity in the PROMIS data, however (Mandel, 1979: 17).

Prison Statistics

Prisoner data are more readily available. The Bureau of the Census reports on persons of Spanish-origin in correctional institutions. Tables 2 and 3 were produced by combining data on persons in institutions with other census data.

Although the quality of the data varies considerably, some individual prison systems also collect data. Perhaps, however, surveys in state correctional facilities and local jails conducted for LEAA between 1972 and 1978 contain the most reliable information on Hispanic prisoners. Race and ethnicity were included in the questionnaires. As Mandel notes, the raw data produced in these studies are excellent; the problem is that

TABLE 1 Arrests by Ethnicity in Illnois, 1975-1976

	White		Black		Mexican and Puerto Rican		Total	
	1975	1977	1975	1977	1975	1977	1975	1977
Crime index arrests	58,896	53,347	60,203	53,346	1,302	944	126,311	113,403
Crimes against persons	3,021	6,838	14,819	8,893	272	219	24,501	18,042
Crimes against property	50,875	46,509	45,384	43,503	1,030	725	101,801	95,361
Murder and voluntary manslaughter	267	256	1,094	809	19	1	1,512	1,253
Forcible rape	333	322	858	700	11	19	1,263	1,124
Aggravated assault, battery and attempted murder	5,310	4,371	4,524	2,067	199	154	10,561	6,712
Robbery	2,111	1,889	8,343	6,317	43	45	11,165	8,953
Burglary	12,139	10,348	9,939	8,273	229	137	23,622	20,065
Theft	35,904	33,193	32,563	32,159	769	535	72,036	68,584
Criminal damage	21,967	11,713	4,247	4,044	221	150	26,516	16,927

SOURCE: Department of Law Enforcement. *Crime in Illinois, 1976* and *Crime in Illinois, 1977*, Crime Statistics Section, Bureau of Identification, Springfield, Illinois.

TABLE 2 Percent Hispanic in Correctional Institutions in States with the Largest Spanish-Origin Populations, 1970

	Percent Hispanic in Federal and State Prisons	Percent Hispanic In Jails and Workhouses	Percent Hispanic in Training schools and Detention Homes	Percent of State's Population Hispanic
California	19.0	15.9	19.4	11.9
Texas	16.0	12.0	18.4	16.4
New York	18.1	14.4	11.3	7.4
Florida	3.6	2.0	1.0	6.0
Illinois	3.8	.5	11.2	3.5
New Mexico	25.8	34.8	55.3	30.3
New Jersey	5.3	2.6	10.7	4.0
Arizona	20.3	17.5	20.7	14.9

SOURCES: U.S. Department of Commerce, *Subject Reports: Persons in Institutions and Other Group Living Quarters*, 1973; U.S. Department of Commerce, *Subject Reports: Persons of Spanish Origin*, 1973; U.S. Department of Commerce, *Characteristics of the Population*, 1973.

TABLE 3   Distribution of Inmates in the United States, by
            Ethnic Group, 1970

	White	Black	Spanish-Origin	Total
Prison s and Reformatories	114,608	80,742	13,596	198,831
Jails and Workhouses	72,591	52,800	8,209	129,189
Training Schools	39,757	24,099	5,287	66,457
Public	33,428	21,894	5,066	57,691
Private	6,329	2,205	281	8,766
Detention Homes	6,754	3,329	765	10,272

SOURCE: U.S. Department of Commerce, *Subject Reports: Persons in
Institutions and Other Group Living Quarters*, 1973.

published summaries do not include Hispanic background. Mandel did
acquire Hispanic data from the 1974 state prisoner survey, however, some
of which is included in Table 4 (Mandel, 1979: 17).

More statistical data on arrests, offense and offender characteristics,
police and court dispositions, and correctional outcomes are necessary
before any conclusions can safely be drawn from the data. The limited
available data, however, suggest several areas of inquiry, such as the
following. Is crime among Spanish-speaking individuals, like crime among
Blacks, more likely to be person-directed and less likely to be property-
directed than crime among whites (cf. Tables 1 and 4)? Do Spanish-
speakers with different national backgrounds tend to have different crime
patterns, for example, Mexicans in the Southwest, Puerto Ricans in New
York, and Cubans in Florida (cf. Table 2)? Are Spanish-speaking juveniles
discriminated against in placement, a smaller percentage being placed in
private and larger percentage in public institutions than for whites or
Blacks (cf. Table 3)? Are Hispanics more prone to drug abuse than other
ethnic groups (cf. Table 4)? Additional official data would also be useful
in determining the reliability of conclusions reached in earlier studies. Is
there support for the conclusion of a 1948 study based on dispositional
figures that police are more likely to make unsupportable arrests of
Chicanos than whites (Lemert and Rosberg, 1948)? Do the offenses of
Spanish-heritage individuals become more like those of the general population the more acculturated they become (Rudoff, 1971)? There are any

TABLE 4   Sentenced Inmates by Offense and Hispanic Origin
1974 LEAA State Prisoner Survey

	Hispanics		Non-Hispanics	
	Number	Percent	Number	Percent
Violent Offenses	3,368	6.2	51,220	93.8
Property Offenses*	4,681	5.1	86,611	94.9
"Other" property offenses	353	3.2	10,624	96.8
Drug or Public Order	3,456	12.3	24,609	87.7
TOTAL	11,858	6.4	173,064	93.6

* Robbery is included in Property Offenses, along with burglary, larceny,
and auto theft.
SOURCE: Jerry Mandel, "Hispanics in the Criminal Justice System—The
Non-existent Problem," *Agenda*, 1979 (9): 19.

number of issues to be raised, but without reliable data, many of the
conclusions must be based on opinion or research in limited areas, often
using small samples. Efforts to improve the quantity and quality of data
are certainly warranted.

INTERACTION WITH THE POLICE

In addition to improvement of statistical data, attention can profitably
be directed toward interaction between Spanish-speaking individuals and
law enforcement, court, and correctional officials.

In 1931, the National Commission on Law Observance and Enforcement indicated that Mexican-Americans, both aliens and citizens, "are
frequently subjected to severe and unequal treatment by those who
administer the laws" (National Commission on Law Observance and
Enforcement, 1931: 243). In 1970, the Civil Rights Commission observed
much the same kind of treatment. In the five southwestern states which
were the subject of the commission's study, allegations that law enforcement officers discriminated against Mexican-Americans were common:

Such discrimination includes more frequent use of force against
Mexican-Americans than against Anglos, discriminatory treatment of

juveniles, and harassment and discourteous treatment toward Mexican-Americans in general. Complaints also were heard that police protection in Mexican-American neighborhoods was less adequate than in other areas. The Commission investigations showed that belief in law enforcement prejudice is wide-spread and is indicative of a serious problem of police-community relations between the police and Mexican-Americans in the Southwest [U.S. Commission on Civil Rights, 1970: 13].

A significant part of the friction in relations is probably related to language. Chevigny suggests that "policemen often take the speaking of a foreign language to be a form of defiance" (1969: 69) and many problems arise simply from law enforcement officers' inability to communicate with Spanish-speakers and resulting misunderstandings. Also, Spanish-speakers are underrepresented among law enforcement personnel (U.S. Commission on Civil Rights, 1970: 83).

Overall, the commission's report painted a "bleak picture" of relationships between Mexican-Americans and criminal justice officials. The commission concluded:

The attitude of Mexican-Americans toward the institutions responsible for the adminstration of justice . . . is distrustful, fearful, and hostile. Police departments, courts, the law itself are viewed as Anglo institutions in which Mexican-Americans have no stake and from which they do not expect fair treatment.

The Commission found that the attitudes of Mexican-Americans are based, at least in part, on the actual experience of injustice . . . There is evidence of police misconduct against Mexican-Americans. In the Southwest, as throughout the nation, remedies for police misconduct are inadequate.

Acts of police misconduct result in mounting suspicion and incite incidents of resistance to officers. These are followed by police retaliation, which results in escalating hostilities [1970: 87].

Similar abuses and misunderstandings have been noted in other areas with heavy concentrations of Spanish-speakers, such as New York City (Chevigny, 1969: 3-29; 69-70) and Chicago (Safford, 1977: 18).

Suggestions are being proposed for improving relationships between police officers and Hispanics. Police officers are encouraged to be aware of cultural traits which might have an affect on interaction. Abad has suggested that if police are aware of the concept of machismo, for example, they can avoid a great deal of difficulty when dealing with young Puerto Ricans who feel they "have to resist authority when approached in a harsh, domineering way" (1974: 587).

Many proposals for improving relationships focus on communication problems. Surveying staff to determine what languages they speak, encouraging bilinguals to apply for positions, and seeking help from community organizations and language departments of colleges and universities are among the recommendations (Nagle and Mata, 1977: 7). The objective is to have someone who speaks the suspect's language readily available.

SPANISH-SPEAKERS IN THE COURTS

The issue of need for an interpreter becomes increasingly critical as the non-English-speaking defendant moves into the courts. It is the non-English speaker's difficulties at this stage which have received more attention from legislative bodies and appellate courts.

Thus far there has been no Supreme Court decision to insure the rights of non-English-speaking defendants in criminal court, in spite of the fact that there are some obvious problem areas in dealing with a non-English-speaking defendant. First, an accused should be notified of the charges against him/her. If that notification is in English, the accused may not understand the nature and consequences of the charge (El Derecho de aviso, 1973). The sixth amendment guarantees the right to counsel. That right may not, however, be meaningful if the accused is unable to communicate with counsel. Further, the sixth amendment guarantees the accused the right to confront and cross-examine witnesses. If those witnesses testify in English which is not translated for the defendant, and particularly if the defendant is unable to adequately consult with counsel, he/she is not in a position to effectively confront and cross-examine. The waiver of rights is also a matter of concern when dealing with a non-English-speaking defendant. Does the defendant who pleads guilty, who waives the right to counsel, or to trial by jury really comprehend the consequences of his/her action? Indeed, there is some question of whether the non-English-or limited-English-speaking defendant can receive a fundamentally fair trial as guaranteed by the due process clause of the fourteenth amendment without the services of an interpreter.

It has largely been left to the judge to evaluate the specific needs, if any, of non-English-speaking defendants, particularly their need for court-appointed interpreters. The only case dealing with this issue reviewed by the Supreme Court held that the decision to appoint an interpreter rests entirely on the discretion of the judge, *Perovich v U.S.* 205 U.S. 86 (1907). Moreover, appellate courts have been reluctant to question the decision of the trial court judges. Trial transcripts do not provide the kind of information necessary to evaluate the defendant's understanding of the proceedings or the adequacy of any translations which may have occurred (Chang and Araujo, 1975: 803).

Nevertheless, some state appellate courts and federal district courts have ruled on cases involving non-English-speaking defendants, and some significant cases can be cited. In New York, an indigent defendant named Rogelio Nieves Negron who did not speak English was assigned counsel who did not speak Spanish. Testimony of witnesses who spoke Spanish was translated; testimony of English-speaking witnesses was not. The defendant, Negron, received only brief periodic summaries of portions of the testimony. Negron was convicted of murder in the second degree. He filed an application for a writ of habeas corpus with the federal court. Judge Bartels granted the writ and indicated that defendants must be informed of the right to a court-appointed interpreter. The second Circuit Court of Appeals affirmed the grant of the writ of habeas corpus, indicating that indigent defendants who are unable to understand English are entitled under the due process clause to assistance of a competent translator throughout the trial, *U.S. ex rel. Negron v. New York*, 434 F.2d 386 (1970).

This decision, however, involved the case of a defendant who spoke no English. Negron's inability to communicate in English was "obvious, not just a possibility" (434 F.2d at 390). In 1973, the First Circuit Court in *United States v. Carrion*, recognized that protection of a defendant's rights may require an interpreter, even if the defendant has some ability to understand and communicate in English, 488 F.2d 12 (1st Cir. 1973). It continued to leave the decision about need for an interpreter in the hands of the judge, but suggested that "precisely because the trial court is entrusted with discretion, it should make unmistakably clear to the defendant who may have a language difficulty that he has the right to a court-appointed interpreter if the court determines one is needed, and, whenever put on notice that there may be some significant language difficulty, the court should make a determination of need" (448 F.2d at 14-15).

The *Carrion* and *Negron* decisions, of course, are legally binding only on courts in the First and Second Circuits. Other federal courts have not clearly supported the right to a court-appointed interpreter. The Tenth Circuit Court of Appeals, in a 1965 decision, indicated that "there is no consitutional right, as such, requiring the assistance of a court-appointed interpreter to supplement the right to counsel. Nor is there a duty to an accused to furnish counsel who can communicate freely with the accused in his native tongue" (*Cervantes v. Cox*, 350 F.2d 855 10th Cir. 1965). Similarly, the Ninth Circuit Court in a case where an interpreter was not requested, and the defendant did communicate in English, held that "it was not abuse of discretion to fail to advise the defendant of availability of interpreter," *U.S. v. Barrios*, 457 F.2d 680 (1972). This court, like courts in the Seventh, *U.S. v Sosa*, 379 F.2d 525 (1967), and Fourth Circuits, *U.S. v. Rodrigues*, 424 F.2d 205 (1970), emphasized the discretion of the trial court.

There are some state courts which have recognized the need for court-appointed interpreters. For example, in *State v. Vasquez*, the Supreme Court of Utah held that the trial court's refusal to provide an interpreter constituted a reversable error, 101 Utah 444, 121 F.2d 903 (1942); and in *Garcia v. State*, the court reversed the conviction because the defendant could not understand evidence presented by the prosecution, 151 Tex. Crim. 593, 201 S.W.2d 574 (1948). Also, some state appellate court decisions indicate that waiving of rights by non-English-or limited-English-speaking defendants is not done knowingly and intelligently, for example, *Parra v. Paige*, 430 P.2d 834 (Okl. Crim. 1967); *Landeros v. State*, P.2d 273 (Okl. Crim. 1971); and *In re* Muraviov, 92 Cal. App. 2d 604, 13 Cal. Rptr. 466 (1961).

In addition, there have been some attempts at the legislative level to insure the rights of non-English-or limited-English-speaking defendants. Thirty-five states have some statutory provision for appointment of interpreters (Safford, 1967: 15). For example, the Illinois law reads:

Wherever any person accused of commiting a felony or misdemeanor is to be tried in any court of this State, the court shall upon its own motion of that of defense or prosection, determine whether the accused is capable of understanding the English language so as to be understood directly by counsel, court or jury. If the court finds the accused incapable of so understanding or so expressing himself, the court shall appoint an interpreter for the accused whom he can understand and who can understand him [Ill. Crim. L. and P. Ch. 38, Sec. 165-11 (1978)].

The California constitution grants "a person unable to understand English who is charged with a crime a right to an interpreter throughout the proceedings" (Cal. Const. Art. 1, Sec. 14, cited in Chang and Araujo, 1975: 820). However, only two states, California and New Mexico, provide for a right to an interpreter in their state constitutions (Chang and Araujo, 1975: 820; Cronheim and Schwartz, 1976: 298).

At the federal level, the Court Interpreters Act (P.L. 95-539) was signed by President Carter on October 29, 1978. This law establishes the right to a certified court interpreter for any party in any civil or criminal action if the court determines that the individual speaks only or primarily a language other than English. Although this law applies only in the federal court system, it serves as a model for state legislation. Thus far, however, it has received little attention and, in fact, the Administrative Office of the United States Courts which is responsible for administration and implementation of P.L. 95-539 is still in the process of estimating the cost of implementing the law (Barcelo, 1979: 25).

The court decisions and state and federal statutes which do exist generally fail to clarify some critical questions with respect to defendants who do not adequately understand English. How is the accused's ability to communicate in and understand English to be evaluated? If an interpreter is to be provided, at what point in the process should he/she be introduced? Does failure to assert the right to an interpreter constitute a waiver of that right? What qualifications must an interpreter possess?

No determination has been made as to the minimum ability of the accused to communicate in English. The appellate courts have repeatedly stated that evaluation of the defendant's ability to communicate and the need for an interpreter is to be left to the trial court judge. The First Circuit Court in the *Carrion* case did indicate that a right to an interpreter exists when the defendant has "obvious difficulty with the language" and further suggested that the complexity of the issues for trial should be considered in making the decision to appoint an interpreter (488 F.2d at 14,15).

Almost nowhere in the statutes or in the court decisions is provision of an interpreter at early stages of the criminal process (arrest, bail setting, preliminary hearing) required. In Illinois, for example, the earliest stage in the criminal process where the law recognizes that there might be a need for an interpreter is at the arraignment (Safford, 1977: 16, 19).

With regard to the non-English-speaking defendant's waiving of rights, particularly the right to an interpreter, Cronheim and Schwartz speak of a "waiver by silence" (1976: 300), indicating that the burden of notifying the court of any language difficulty is often placed on the defendant and his counsel. The Second Circuit Court implied disapproval of this "waiver by silence," pointing out that the standard for a constitutional waiver is that it be "an intentional relinquishment or abandonment of a known right." In the *Negron* case, the defendant had not waived his right to an interpreter, said the court, by his failure to request those services (434 F.2d at 387, 390). Again, however, the scope of the Second Circuits decision is limited.

The language interpreter statutes and court decisions say very little about qualifications of interpreters. California does provide that judges may use examinations to insure the competency of interpreters. In most states this is not done, however, In Illinois, for example, the courts have found interpreters incompetent in only a few cases, and those involved translation of testimony of witnesses where confusion caused by the interpreter's incompetence was obvious (Safford, 1977: 26,27). Convictions have resulted in cases where the interpreter was a law enforcement officer involved in the investigation and arrest, the complainant, a witness, an employee of the prosecutor's office, and illiterate codefendant (Cronheim and Schwartz, 1976: 307; Safford, 1977: 25, 26). The Court Interpreters Act requires the Director of the Administrative Office of the United States Courts to establish a program to certify individuals who may serve as interpreters in Federal District Court. A certification process has not yet been established, however (Barcelo, 1979: 25).

The similarity between the situation of the person who is "incompetent" to stand trial because of language difficulties and the person who is incompetent for "mental" reasons has been noted by several observers. The Second Circuit Court pointed out that Negron's language problem was "as debilitating to his ability to participate in the trial as a mental disease or defect. But it was more readily 'curable' than any mental disorder" (434 F.2d at 390). The Supreme Court has indicated, in discussing mental incompetence, that due process requires that the defendant have "sufficient present ability to consult with his lawyer with a reasonable degree of rational understanding," *U.S. v. Dusky*, 362 U.S. 402 (1960). The Supreme Court has further held that when there is an indication that the

defendant is mentally incompetent, the trial court must stop the proceedings and conduct a hearing to make such a determination, *Pate v.
Robinson*, 383, U.S. 375 (1966). While the relevance of these cases to the
non-English speakers. The Ninth Circuit Court had held that school dis-
tricts are under no obligation to provide compensatory language instruction and that there is no right to a bilingual education. The Supreme
Court, however, held that forcing non-English-speaking children to attend
classes taught only in English denies them a meaningful opportunity to
participate in the public education program and violates the Civil Rights
Act of 1964, which prohibits discrimination in programs receiving federal
financial assistance, *Lau v. Nichols*, 414 U.S. 563 (1974). Likewise, Chang
and Araujo suggest that requiring court proceedings be in English without
provision of an interpreter constitutes discrimination. "When a non-
English speaking defendant is denied an interpreter it would seem unden-
iable that discriminatory state action exists" (1975: 805, 808).

CORRECTIONAL PROGRAMMING FOR SPANISH SPEAKERS

In the area of corrections, the literature has several relevant references
to class and cultural differences between the change-agent and the client
which hamper communication and effective treatment. "Beyond some
recognition of some ethnic 'differences,'" however, "little is done in
corrections to assess the effect of the traditional incarceration process and
resocialization techniques" on Hispanics (Rudoff, 1971: 224). "Corrections itself appears to have gone on the assumption that all offenders are
alike and has made little differentiation among them. Any variations in
treatment have centered mainly around psychological rather than cultural
differences" (Sanfilippo and Wallach, 1967: 65).

Working with Spanish-heritage individuals is often particularly trouble-
some for the therapist. "The intimacies necessary in therapy are traditionally avoided" by Hispanics. "One simply does not discuss one's mother . . .
or one's father with other people. Problems . . . are also avoided. The
therapist represents an authority figure and is viewed with suspicion and
distrust . . . Finally, there is fear of acculturation itself . . . , the fear that

therapy will pull him away from his . . . identity and that he might lose the acceptance of his people." The Anglo, by contrast, more readily learns and accepts "the role of the client" (Rudoff, 1971: 236). Group therapy is an especially sensitive issue. Not only do Hispanics often resent attempts to force them to reveal their "inner selves" in front of others, many reportedly experience embarrassment regarding their inability to speak English well (Bullington, 1977: 133, 134).

Perhaps language problems combined with problems resulting from cultural traits explain, at least in part, why there is an observed tendency for Hispanics involved in psychotherapy to receive intensive verbally oriented treatment less often and drug-oriented intervention more often then Anglo clients (Henggler and Tavormina, 1978: 98).

Corrections officials might be well-advised to concentrate their efforts on behalf of Spanish-speaking offenders in the area of education. New techniques for bilingual instruction are being developed which can probably be incorporated into correctional programs. Since 1970, the Spanish Curricula Development Center has been developing and producing instructional materials needed in bilingual programs (Hartner, 1977). In 1976, the Office of Education contracted for a study of the state of bilingual material development which was recently released, and nine materials development centers have been created (National Advisory Council on Bilingual Education, 1976: 31). Thus, while the U.S. Commission on Civil Rights concluded that minorities, including Hispanics, "do not obtain the benefits of public education at a rate equal to that of their Anglo classmates" (1971: 41), significant advances have been made in bilingual/bicultural education, especially since the *Lau v. Nichols* decision.

Emphasis on educational programs for Spanish-speakers would also be in keeping with current trends in the field of corrections. A considerable amount of money is spent each year on correctional programs. The total amount spent on corrections education by both federal and nonfederal institutions is approximately $546 million. Focus on correctional education has increased in recent years. Relative to other "rehabilitation" programs, education has become a high priority. Also, education has come to include social education as well as academic and vocational education. "Social education programs is on helping (offenders) understand themselves, providing insight, developing realistic self-concepts, gaining appropriate skills and inter-personal relationships, and coping with problems they must face . . . as consumers, family members, employees and responsible citizens" (U.S. Department of Health, Education and Welfare, 1977: 46).

Some corrections education programs aimed at Spanish-speaking offenders do exist. For example, there is a correctional institution which includes a program for Spanish-speaking juveniles funded under the Elementary and Secondary Education Act., Title I, at Rikers Island in New York (Griggs, 1975); the Texas State Department of Corrections has an Adult Bilingual Laboratory and Learning Center at Huntsville (Texas State Department of Corrections, 1973); and the Illinois Department of Corrections has a bilingual/bicultural program at Stateville (Campos, 1978.) These programs, however, seem to be developing largely independent of one another and based more on general recognition of need on awareness of the existence, experience, and effectiveness of other bilingual corrections education programs.

Corrections officials concerned with the plight of Spanish-speaking, and other non-English-speaking, offenders must be kept abreast of relevant developments in correctional education and in bilingual/bicultural education in particular. The number of Spanish-speakers in corrections programs is increasing, and educational theorists have concluded that non-English speakers learn better in a bilingual/bicultural setting because of the positive effect the setting has on the cognitive and affective domain (National Advisory Council on Bilingual Education, 1976: 18).

Further, corrections personnel working with Spanish-speakers should be given the oppurtunity to learn the language, something about the history and values of their clients (e.g., Mexican, Puerto Rican), and the "problems faced by migrants who relocate physically and culturally" (Knowlton, 1967: 26; Monserrat, 1967: 57). They "should be aware of the traditional patterns of etiquette followed by this group of people" and even of "differences between and within the various groups of Spanish-heritage persons" (Chaves, 1976: 219; 30-31).

The "Seminar on the Implications of Cultural Differences" for Corrections indicated:

That an understanding of social and cultural characteristics of minority group members will lead correctional agencies and the educational institutions which are training personnel for corrections to develop more effective curriculum content, training methods, and utilization and recruitment of personnel . . . Planning and development which take account of cultural differences can help greatly in bringing about the rehabilitation of offenders who come from minority groups in our society [Sanfilippo and Wallach, 1967: 68].

If corrections programs ignore the existence of language and cultural differences, "people will continue not to respond to the treatment, to the rehabilitation, or to whatever program we're trying to give them" (Montez, 1967: 12).

SUMMARY

Spanish-speaking residents of the United States are frequently faced with socioeconomic and emotional pressures often associated with crime. Their income and educational levels are below average and residing in an unfamiliar culture deprives them of "familiar cues and controls." The subtle, unspoken, conventions that one has learned from childhood are changed and familiar gestures take on new meanings; many of the old experiences from which one derived satisfaction and support are no longer there" (Guthrie, 1975: 98).

The actual amount of crime in the Spanish-speaking community, however, has not been accurately determined. Statistical data is limited. More data must be collected if significant questions regarding the nature and extent of crime in the Spanish-speaking community are to be answered.

Information presently available suggests that there is need for considerable improvement in the handling of Spanish-speaking offenders. Spanish-heritage individuals are often distrustful of law enforcement officials, and law enforcement officials often misunderstand and sometimes mistreat Hispanic suspects. Recommendations for improving police-Hispanic-community relations should be given serious attention.

The rights of the Spanish-speaking, and other non-English-speaking, defendants in court have been considered by some appellate courts and legislative bodies. The non-English-speaking defendant's right to counsel, to confront and cross-examine witnesses, and to a fundamentally fair trial, some have concluded, require the presence of an interpreter. The Supreme Court, however, has not ruled on the rights of non-English-speaking defendants; and several critical areas remain unclear.

Spanish-speaking defendants who are found guilty present a special problem to correctional officials. If their situations are to be "corrected," programs must be designed to meet their needs. Traditional therapy is often difficult to apply to Spanish-heritage individuals. There have, however, been some significant developments in bilingual/bicultural education which might profitably be applied in correctional programs. Also, correctional personnel must be made sensitive to cultural differences.

It would appear that in years to come the criminal justice system (police, courts, and corrections) will be forced to seriously consider the unique perspectives and needs of Spanish-speaking individuals. Their numbers are growing rapidly. Attention to their rights seems to be increasing. Hispanics are becoming more politically aware and aggressive; they have formed several organizations, including La Raza Unida, the Political Association of Spanish Organizations, and the Mexican-American Political Association (U.S. Commission on Civil Rights, 1970: xiii; "It's Your Turn in the Sun," 1978). Hopefully, the sooner the issues involved are confronted, the sooner they can be resolved.

CASES

BARRIOS v. U.S., 457 F2d 680 (9th Cir. 1972)
CARRION v. U.S., 488 F.2d 12 (1st Cir. 1973)
CERVANTES v. COX, F.2d (10th Cir. 1965)
DUSKY v. U.S., 362 U.S. 402 (1960)
GARCIA v. STATE, 151 Tex. Crim. 593, 501 S.W.2d 574 (1948)
LANDEROS v. STATE, P.2d 273 (Okl. Crim. 1971)
LAU v. NICHOLS, 414 U.S. 563 (1974)
MARAVIOV, *In Re* 192 Cal. App. 2a 604, 13 Cal. Rptr. 466 (1961)
NEGRON, U.S., *ex rel.* v. NEW YORK, 434 F.2d 386 (1970)
PARRA v. PAIGE, 430 P.2d 834 (Okl. Crim. 1967)
PATE v. ROBINSON, 383 U.S. 375 (1966)
PEROVICH v. U.S., 205 U.S. 86 (2nd Cir. 1907)
RODRIGUES v. U.S., 424 F.2d 205 (4th Cir. 1970)
SOSA v. U.S., 379 F.2d 525 (7th Cir. 1967)
VASQUEZ v. STATE, 101 Utah 444, 121 P.2d 903 (1942)

REFERENCES

Abad, V., J. Ramos, and E. Boyce, (1974) "A model for delivery of mental health services to Spanish-speaking minorities." *American Journal of Orthopsychiatry*, 44: 584-595.

Barcelo, C. (1979) "The Court Interpreters Act—A step towards equal justice." *Agenda* 9: 21-25; 33.

Bullington, B. (1977) *Heroin Use in the Barrio*. Lexington, MA: D.C. Heath.

Campos, L. (1978) Personal interview.

Chang, W.B.C. and M.V. Araugo, (1975) "Interpreters for the defense: Due process for the non-speaking defendant." *California Law Review*, 68; 801-823.

Chaves, F. J. (1976) "Counseling offenders of Spanish heritage." *Federal Probation*, 40: 29-33.

Chevigny, P. (1969) *Police Power: Police Abuses in New York City*. New York: Pantheon.

Cronheim, A. J. and A. H. Schwartz (1976) "Non-English-speaking persons in the criminal justice system: Current state of the law." *Cornell Law Review*, 61: 289-311.

Department of Law Enforcement (1977) *Crime in Illinois 1977*. Springfield, IL: Crime Statistics Section, Bureau of Identification.

——— (1976) *Crime in Illinois 1976*. Springfield, IL: Crime Statistics Section, Bureau of Identification.

"El derecho de aviso: Due process and bilingual notice." (1973) *Yale Law Journal*, 83: 385-400.

Griggs, S. (1975) *Program for Adolescents in Corrective Institutions—Rikers Island*. Brooklyn: New York City Board of Education. (ERIC Document Reproduction Service No. ED 138 681)

Guthrie, G. M. (1975) "A behavioral analysis of cultural learning." In R. W. Brislin et al. (eds.) *Cross-Cultural Perspectives on Learning*. New York: Wiley.

Hartner, E. (1977) "How we develop bilingual instructional materials—Spanish Curricula Development Center." *Educational Leadership*, 35: 42-46.

Henggeler, S. W. and J. B. Tavormina (1978) "The children of Mexican-American migrant workers: A population at risk?" *Journal of Abnormal Child Psychology*, 6: 97-106.

Hernandez, J., L. Estrada, and D. Alvirez (1973) "Census data and the problem of conceptually defining the Mexican-American population." *Social Science Quarterly*, 53: 671-687.

Illinois State (1979) *Illinois Criminal Law and Procedure for 1978*. St. Paul, MN: West.

"It's your turn in the sun." (1978) *Time* (October 16): 48-52; 55; 58; 61.

Knowlton, C. S. (1967) "Spanish-speaking people of the southwest." In R. K. McNickle (ed.) *Differences that Make a Difference: Papers Presented at a Seminar on the Implications of Cultural Differences for Corrections*. Washington, DC: Joint Commission on Correctional Manpower Training.

Lemert, E. M. and J. Rosberg (1948) "The administration of justice to minority groups Los Angeles County." In R.L. Beals et al. (eds.) *University of California Publications in Culture and Society, II.* Berkeley and Los Angeles: University of California Press.

Mandel, J. (1979) "Hispanics in the criminal justice system—the "non-existant" problem. *Agenda* 9: 16-20.

Monserrat, J. (1967) "Puerto Ricans." In R. K. McNickle (ed.) *Differences that Make a Difference: Paper Presented at a Seminar on the Implications of Cultural Differences for Corrections.* Washington DC: Joint Commission on Correctional Manpower and Training.

Nagle, B. and J. Mata (1977) "Improving police contact with non-English speaking peoples." *Law Enforcement News* (December 20): 1.

National Advisory Council on Bilingual Education (1976) *Second Annual Report* Washington, DC: Interamerica.

National Commission on Law Observance and Enforcement (1974) "Report on crime and the foreign born: 1931." In C. E. Cortes (advisory ed.) *The Mexican American and the Law.* New York: Arno Press.

Rudoff, A. (1971) "The incarcerated Mexican-American delinquent." *Journal of Criminal Law, Criminology, and the Police Science*, 62: 224-238.

Safford, J. B. (1977) "No comprendo: The non-English-speaking defendant and the criminal process." *Journal of Criminal Law*, 68: 15-30.

Sanfilippo, R. and J. Wallach (1967) "Cultural differences: Implications for corrections." In R. K. McNickle (ed.) *Differences that Make a Difference: Papers Presented at a Seminar on the Implications of Cultural Differences for Corrections.* Washington, DC: Joint Commission on Correctional Manpower and Training.

Statistical Analysis Center (n.d.) *IUCR User's Guide and Codebooks.* Springfield: Illinois Law Enforcement Commission.

Texas Department of Corrections (1973) *Adult Reading.* Huntsville, TX: Bilingual Laboratories and Learning Center.

Towner, P. (1978) Personal Interview.

U.S. Commission on Civil Rights (1978) *Social Indicators of Equality for Minorities and Women.* Washington, DC: Government Printing Office.

——— (1974) *Counting the Forgotten: The 1970 Census Count of Persons of Spanish Speaking Background in the United States: A Report.* Washington, DC: Government Printing Office.

——— (1971) *The Unfinished Education.* Washington DC: Government Printing Office.

——— (1970) *Mexican Americans and the Administration of Justice in the Southwest.* Washington DC: Government Printing Office.

U.S. Department of Commerce, Bureau of the Census (1975) *Persons of Spanish Origin in the United States: Current Reports, 1975.* Washington, DC: Government Printing Office.

——— (1973a) *Detailed Characteristics: United States Summary, 1973.* Washington, DC: Government Printing Office.

——— (1973b) *Subject Reports: Persons in Institutions and Other Group Living Quarters, 1973*. Washington, DC: Government Printing Office.

——— (1973c) *Subject Reports: Persons of Spanish Origin, 1973*. Washington, DC: Government Printing Office.

U.S. Department of Health, Education, and Welfare (1977) *A Review of Corrections Education Policy*. Washington, DC: MetaMetrics (ERIC Document Reproduction Service No. ED 141 585)

III.

Empirical Examination of Racial Bias

Possible inequities in the treatment afforded members of national minority groups are examined empirically in this section. Bynum's research explores parole decision making to determine if American Indians are more likely, compared to whites, to be unfavorably reviewed. Bynum argues that this kind of decision making is of low visibility that is, normally not subject to a formal review process. In addition, parole judgments are based on highly discretionary, subjective factors, rather than formally specified criteria. Bynum concludes that these conditions can allow the biases of individual parole board members to influence the outcomes of parole hearings.

The sample was selected from a cohort of offenders admitted to a state prison system in an upper plains state having a large population of American Indians. Offenders' sentence lengths were combined with the amount of time served to yield a single measure of punishment severity. One of the several interesting findings of this study was that although American Indians served significantly higher proportions of their sentences, they also received shorter sentences for one category of offense (burglary). Saliently, when legal and social factors were included in the analysis, American Indians still were found to serve significantly higher proportions of their sentences. Thus, Bynum's findings strongly support this thesis, although he notes other possible interpretations which take into account several factors, including the possibility that parole boards seek to equalize the amount of actual time served by American Indians and white offenders.

In his investigation of the use of deadly force, Fyfe examines whether police officers are more prone to use their firearms during encounters with Blacks and Hispanics. Hypotheses tested include two competing perspectives concerning the overrepresentation of minorities as victims of police shooting deaths. The first stresses that Blacks and certain minorities have disporportionately higher arrest rates for crimes of violence while the other argues that "police have one trigger finger for whites and another for Blacks." The data source consisted of New York City Police Department records in which officers reported discharging weapons and/or being the subject of "serious assault" during the years 1971-1975.

Among the many findings reported in this article include the fact that Black males in all age groups are considerably more likely to become police shooting opponents than are their white/Hispanic contemporaries. Further, Blacks made up a disproportionate share of shooting opponents reportedly armed with guns and engaged in robberies when police intervened. Possible inaccuracies and other problems associated with the several data sources used in this study, including the veracity of police reports, are indicated and discussed. Within the specified limits of the data, Fyfe notes that little evidence was obtained to support the contention that Blacks are more likely than whites to be shot in less serious situations. The author concludes that Blacks are the mode among New York's police shooting opponents because they are also the mode among the lower socioeconomic groups which most frequently participate in the types of activity likely to precipitate extreme police-citizen violence.

Schuster, comparing differences between Black and white violent juvenile offenders, found that violent youth of both races were far more likely than other youth to be from low socioeconomic (SES) backgrounds, with Blacks even more likely than their white counterparts to be from such backgrounds. The data included all youths born in years 1956 through 1960 who had been arrested for at least one violent crime. Black juvenile involvement in violent offenses exceeded Black representation in the geographical unit (Franklin County, Ohio) under study. Noting a strong relationship between SES and criminal involvement, the author suggests that Black overrepresentation may be due to the fact that Blacks also are highly overrepresented in Franklin County's low-SES population; analysis of the relationship between SES and race showed a "remarkably high" statistical correlation.

Differences between Black and white violent offenders were found to be comparatively minor. For example, white violent offenders averaged slightly more arrests than Blacks, recidivism was about equal for the two groups, and white youth were more likely than Black youth to be chronic (five or more arrests) repeaters. Black youth were more likely to have multiple serious violent arrests, although the relationship between race and type of violent offense was weak. Very few offenders, Black or white, could be characterized as truly violent delinquents. The great bulk of arrests for both races was for nonviolent crime and the majority of violent arrests were for less serious violent offenses of simple assault, sexual imposition, and unarmed robbery. Pointing out that important knowledge gaps exist in regard to violent delinquents, Schuster stresses the continuing need for empirical explorations of race and crime among these offenders. For example, he notes that the use, in his own study, of arrest data has obvious drawbacks, including the fact that racial overrepresentation may be related to prejudicial police handling of Blacks.

Feyerherm's article focuses upon the processing of juveniles referred for status offenses in 10 California counties. Examining both the intake decisions by county probation offices and the dispositions eventually provided by the juvenile courts, the analysis shows that minority youth, both Black and Mexican American, are more likely to receive formal treatment by the juvenile justice system. Minority youth are more likely to have a request for a formal petition filed by the county probation department and are more likely to receive a sentence of formal super-vision.

When their patterns are examined separately for each county, notable differences in processing occur. Several patterns are identified which differ across counties, which indicate that a search for evidence of racial differentiation must take into account the possibilities of different patterns of offense type, decision point, and county. In particular, analysis of differential processing must take into account the combined effects of several stages of decision making. Such combinations can serve as a positive feedback system to amplify the differential effects of processing at each stage.

4

PAROLE DECISION MAKING AND NATIVE AMERICANS

Tim Bynum

Assistant Professor
School of Criminal Justice
Michigan State University

The investigation of the influence of race upon the imposition of criminal sanctions has long been a favored topic for criminological research. This interest is rooted in two major theoretical traditions: the conflict approach and the labelling perspective. Conflict theorists have generally emphasized the importance of social and economic status and power relationships in the imposition of criminal sanctions. The criminal sanction is viewed from this perspective as a mechanism through which those who threaten the interests of the status quo may be controlled. As power is distributed along class and race dimensions in American society, the threats to this existing power structure are also seen by conflict theorists to be identified through racial and economic characteristics. Thus, members of lower economic classes and particularly those of racial minorities are seen as being subject to more frequent and more severe criminal penalties. Turk (1969: 68) expresses this expected relationship in propositional form: "As the power difference favoring the enforcers increases, the probability of criminalization of the opposition increases." In addition, members of this socially disadvantaged group are viewed as less able to resist the application of criminal penalties as are more affluent individuals. Since these

AUTHOR'S NOTE: I would like to thank Kurt Siedschlaw who collected the data used in this article and Gary Cordner for his comments concerning the analysis of these data.

groups have fewer resources to fight arrest, prosecution, and conviction, criminal justice agencies are less concerned about making mistakes in the handling of these cases (Chambliss and Seidman, 1971). Thus, Hepburn (1978) argues that law enforcement agencies are more likely to employ Packer's (1964) crime control model, which emphasizes the speedy and efficient processing of criminal cases, with blacks and the "due process model," emphasizing the rights of the individual, with whites.

The labelling perspective, while creating similar expectations concerning the application of the criminal sanction, employs a different explanation of these relationships. While less concerned with relationships of power and domination, the labelling perspective focuses on societal reaction to deviant behavior. The meaning and seriousness of individual action is not so much a property of the act itself but lies in the type and degree of reaction to this behavior. Since, from this perspective, patterns of acceptable behavior are viewed as being determined through a culture conflict process, certain groups are more likely to have their behaviors become subject to the criminal sanction than others. Thus, lower class individuals and members of racial minorities are seen as having a higher "categorical risk" of not only being involved in the criminal justice system but also of receiving more severe sanctions as a function of this group membership (Schur, 1973). Stereotypes concerning group membership are viewed as heavily influencing criminal justice decision makers in their disposition concerning lower class and minority individuals.

In addition to the expectations generated from these theoretical perspectives, we also can point to the potential impact of race in criminal justice decisions that are characterized as low-visibility types of decisions. Such decisions are those that are typically without a formal review process, highly discretionary, and do not have formal decision criteria. The police decision to arrest is often characterized in this manner. In most cases, the decision to arrest is greatly influenced by the feeling of the officer concerning the appropriateness of this form of official response. In a similar manner, the prosecutor's decision to charge is also influenced by his perception of the appropriateness of the charge and is undoubtedly influenced by many factors other than case-relevant variables (Cole, 1970). In these highly discretionary decisions, personal values, attitudes, and biases are seen as at least having the potential of greatly influencing the outcome.

The decision to grant early release from prison on parole can also be described as a low-visibility decision. Stanley (1976) characterizes this decision as being made on highly subjective judgments by parole board members and with inconsistent rationale for release or continued incarceration. Prior research has emphasized the importance of a wide range of factors in parole release decisions. Hawkins (1971), in a study of parole board decision making in New York, found little consistency between the stated criteria upon which parole board members indicated that their decisions were made and the actual behavior of the parole authority. While parole board members stated that the most important criteria was the seriousness of the offense, Hawkins's study revealed that decisions were actually most influenced by the inmate's poor behavior at the parole hearing, the affect the release would have on prison morale, and the inmate's poor attitude toward authority.

In his analysis of the length of time served prior to parole release, Scott (1974) found, not surprisingly, that the most important factor was the type (i.e., seriousness) of offense. However, Scott's study also reports the severity of punishment to be negatively associated with socioeconomic status, education, intelligence, and being married, while positive associations were reported with age and the number of violations of prison rules. Dawson (1966), in a study of a parole board activities in Kansas, Michigan, and Wisconsin, also points to the wide range of justifications that can be employed to grant release or to continue imprisonment. While each of these studies has pointed to the subjective nature of parole board decision making, none has specifically addressed the influence of the inmate's race upon these low-visibility decisions.[1] Given the nature of these decisions and the expectations from the conflict and labelling perspectives, it is reasonable to hypothesize that race may exert substantial influence in the decision to grant early release from prison. The present analysis will explore this relationship.

There have been a wide range of studies investigating the impact of race and ethnic identification on decisions rendered at various points throughout the criminal justice system. Two studies (Hagan, 1974; Hindelang, 1969) summarizing this literature concluded that although race is generally associated with severity of sanction (with minorities receiving more severe punishments), when legal factors such as prior offenses and type of offense are controlled, little evidence of differential treatment is noted. Such conclusions are however, far from unanimous, as a number of studies continue to report the existence of discriminatory treatment of minorities in each stage of the criminal justice process. Thornberry (1973), in a study of juvenile court dispositions in Philadelphia, found that blacks were more likely to be institutionalized than were whites with similar characteristics. Ferdinand and Luchterhand (1970) also found evidence of racial differences in the imposition of sanctions by the juvenile court. Chiricos (1972), in a study of the factors associated with the withholding of a formal adjudication of guilt for Florida probationers, also discovered evidence of the strength of race in this decision. While introducing controls for a wide range of legal and social variables, these authors indicated that blacks were more likely than whites to receive an adjudication of guilt regardless of the type of offense and number of prior convictions. Thus, they were led to conclude that "race plays a consistent and significant role in the determination of who receives and who avoids this criminal stigma." Evidence of differential treatment on the basis of race has also been noted in the police decision to arrest. Hepburn (1978), in his study of the issuance of warrants, found that nonwhites are more likely to be arrested under circumstances that would result in the refusal of a criminal warrant.

While the results of these research efforts are instructive, three additional studies are particularly germane to the present analysis. Peterson and Friday (1975) argue that if discriminatory treatment exists in the criminal justice system, it is most likely to be found in the processes that are less visible. In the above studies that reported the importance of race in criminal justice outcomes, those by Hepburn (1978) and Chiricos et al. (1972) can be described as dealing with low-visibility decisions. In their own study of the early release of youthful offenders from incarceration, Peterson and Friday (1975) found that whites were significantly more likely to be granted "shock probation." This early release from prison, while operating under judicial and probation authorities instead of through an administrative process, can nonetheless be seen as similar to parole parole release in its low-visibility nature.

While most of the studies thus far discussed have focused on the differences in the treatment afforded blacks as compared to whites, little research attention has been focused on the criminal justice outcomes received by other racial minorities. However, in some sections of the country other groups, particularly Chicanos and Native Americans, comprise a significant proportion of the minority population. The focus of the present analysis will be the treatment afforded Native Americans in the decision to release on parole; as such, two studies that concerned Native Americans in the criminal justice system are of particular interest. Hall and Simkus (1975) analyzed the type of sentence imposed on both white and Native American defendants in a state with a significant Indian population. These authors report a significant relationship between being an Indian and the type of sentence imposed with 76% of all Indian defendants receiving a sentence of incarceration as compared to 59% of white defendants.[2] When relevant legal and social factors were controlled, the strength of this relationship diminished but was not elminated from influence in the type of sentence imposed.

Of major importance for present concerns is a study by Swift and Bickel (1974) conducted for the Bureau of Social Science Research of the parole treatment of Native Americans in the Federal Prison System in 1973 and 1974. Within crime categories, Native Americans were found to serve 15% more time in prison prior to being released on parole. However, it was also reported that Indians have received longer sentences than whites; thus, this apparent discrepancy in parole treatment may in fact be a result of differential treatment in court. In addition, this report did not include additional factors concerning major infractions while in prison or criminal history that may also conceivably influence release from prison. The present analysis will incorporate controls for these legal factors and additional social characteristics in an attempt to more completely address the issue of parole release and Native Americans.

DATA ANALYSIS

The data used in this analysis come from an upper plains state with a relatively large population of Native Americans. The sample was selected from a cohort of offenders admitted to the state prison system during 1970. Data were gathered in 1976, thereby allowing sufficient time for most offenders admitted during that year to have received full parole consideration or have been released due to sentence expiration. There were 255 offenders who were admitted to this prison system during the period of study and only 17 had sentences too long to be considered for analysis. Second, crime categories were excluded that had very few cases or were so unique (e.g., child molesting) that their inclusion may have distorted the results. Finally those offenders serving sentences for which they would not receive parole consideration were excluded from the analysis. This sample reduction left 137 offenders of which amount 54, or 39%, were Native Americans. This remaining group was composed primarily of offenders convicted of property crimes. Of the 83 non-Indian offenders, 2 were Black and the remainder were white.

Instead of viewing the parole decision in a discrete manner, this analysis proposes a consideration of this decision in a more continuous fashion.

TABLE 1   Mean Proportion of Sentence Served

	All Cases (N=137)	Burglary Cases (N=43)
Indian	.86*	.84*
Non-Indian	.75	.64

* p ≤ .01

That is, how much of the imposed sentence was served prior to parole being granted. This procedure has several advantages over analysis based on whether an individual was paroled or not. Since most offenders receive some form of conditional release prior to sentence expiration, analysis based on "if" release was granted may mask racial differences that may emerge in a consideration of "when" release was granted. Second, this procedure overcomes the difficulty of the Swift and Bickel (1974) study by combining time served with sentence imposed to gain a single measure of severity of punishment. A final advantage of this approach is that it acts as a crude control of the seriousness of offense. An offender who serves two years of a four-year sentence has served longer than one who has served 18 months of a two-year sentence. However, the second offender has clearly been punished more severely. By conceptualizing the dependent variable in this manner, the somewhat obvious finding that the seriousness of the offense is the best predictor of the length of incarceration is avoided.

Two dependent variables were employed in this analysis: proportion of sentence served[3] and length of sentence imposed. Table 1 presents the bivariate relationship between being a Native American and the proportion of sentence served. For all cases in the sample, Indians served an average of 86% of their sentence while non-Indian offenders served 75%. A difference of proportions test reveals this difference to be statistically significant at the .01 level. Since this group of cases included a wide range of types of offenses, a second analysis was performed on only those offenders convicted for burglary. There were 43 individuals who were serving sentences for this offense and 19, or 44%, were Native Americans. Table 1 indicates that for this homogeneous group of offenders, Indian offenders served on the average 84% of their sentence while non-Indian offenders served 64%. Once again this difference is significant at the .01 level.

Table 2 reveals the mean length of the sentence imposed for Indians and non-Indian offenders. It is interesting and somewhat surprising to note that sentences imposed on Indian defendants are significantly shorter than those received by non-Indians. While this finding bears little importance in all-cases category due to the range of offense type, it is clear that for offenses of burglary, the mean sentence imposed for Native Americans is significantly less ($p < .01$) than that received by non-Indians.

While these bivariate relationships are interesting, they only serve to beg the question of what happens to this relationship when controls for various legal factors and social characteristics are introduced. Table 3 presents the standardized Betas for the regression analysis using proportion of sentence served as the dependent variable. The number of prior felony convictions and the number of major infractions while incarcerated were introduced as "legal" variables while the age, educational level, and race of the individual were used as social factors.[4] In the regression analysis using all cases, the relationship between being an Indian and proportion of sentence served remains significant ($p < .05$). In addition, the age of the offender and the number of major infractions are also significantly positively related to the proportion of time served. Although not significant, the coefficients for the prior convictions and education variables are in the "expected" directions.

Of major importance in Table 3 is the analysis of the reduced sample of burglary cases. The results in this one case type indicate that strong importance of Indian status on the proportion of time served, followed by the impact of major infrations. With an R^2 value of .40, it is apparent that these factors are of major importance in the proportion of sentence served prior to release.

A similar regression procedure was performed using the length of sentence imposed as the dependent variable. Table 4 presents the results of this analysis. Although, the amount of variance explained in length of sentence is quite small for both the all cases and burglary sample, the strongest and only significant relationship noted is between being an Indian and length of sentence. Native Americans received significantly lower sentences even when the affect of the number of prior offenses was controlled.

The analysis of the proportion of sentence served in the burglary sample was further pursued to investigate the interrelationships between the explanatory variables. Figure 1 presents the results of this path-analytic approach. Initially noted are the strong relationships between proportion of sentence served and being an Indian and major infractions.

TABLE 2   Mean Length of Sentence Imposed
(in months)

	All Cases (N=137)	Burglary Cases (N=43)
Indian	18.6*	16.2**
Non-Indian	26.5	24.8

  *P <   .001
**P ≤   .01

TABLE 3   Regression Results: Proportion of
Sentence Served

	All Cases (N=139)	Burglary Cases (N=43)
Indian	.17*	.42*
Age	.24*	.19
Education	-.12	-.09
Major Infractions	.24*	.34*
Prior Convictions	.17	.20
	$R^2 = .23$	$R^2 = .40$

*p < .05

TABLE 4   Regression Results: Length of
Sentence Imposed

	All Cases (N=131)	Burglary Cases (N=43)
Indian	-.27*	-.36*
Age	-.09	-.07
Education	.11	-.16
Prior convictions	.17	.18
	$R^2 = .12$	$R^2 = .16$

*p < .05

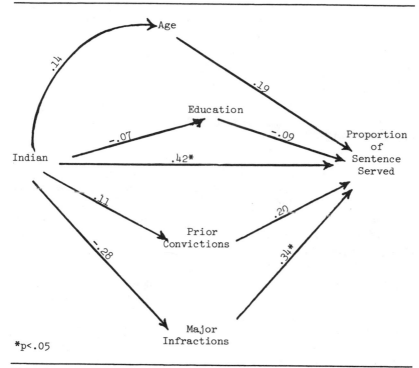

Figure 1   Path Diagram Proportion of Time Served Burglary

One might expect that there may be an indirect effect of racial indentification upon the dependent variable through major infractions. While there is a fairly strong Beta weight (.28) for the relationship between race and major infractions, it is in a negative direction. That is, while those having major infractions are likely to serve a longer proportion of their sentence, these individuals are also less likely to be Native Americans. The indirect effect through prior offenses indicates that Indians are more likely to have prior convictions and those having prior convictions are likely to serve a longer proportion of their sentence; however, neither of these relationships is statistically significant. Similarly, Indians were less likely to have a higher educational level and those having a higher education were more likely to serve a smaller proportion of their sentence, but again neither of these relationships was statistically significant nor did they have large standardized Betas. From these data, it appears that the race of the inmate exerts a strong and independent effect upon the proportion of time he will be incarcerated prior to release.

DISCUSSION

The conflict and labelling perspective hypothesize that criminal justice sanctions will be more severely imposed on racial minorities. It has further been suggested that if discriminatory treatment in the criminal justice system exists, it is most likely to occur in decisions that are highly discretionary and of low visibility. While support for these expectations has not been overwhelming in regard to the treatment of blacks in the criminal justice system, the present analysis tends to confirm the existence of differential treatment of Native Americans in the decision to release on parole in this state.

Just as the conflict and labelling approaches may offer different explanations for similar findings, the present set of outcomes does not lend itself to easy and direct interpretation. The first issue that should be noted is that although the model described in Figure 1 has several significant relationships, it is clear that 60% of the variance in the dependent variable remains unexplained. With a larger sample with a greater number of variables that may be relevant to parole board decisions, such as having a job plan or community support or hostility, this level of uncertainty may be reduced.

With this caveat in mind, the second major issue concerning these findings may be addressed: What is it about being a Native American that induces the parole board to impose a more severe sanction upon these individuals. Do Indians, in fact, have a higher recidivism rate and the parole board follows a policy of predictive restraint? Are Native Americans more likely to be seen by parole board members as more in need of "prison treatment?" Hawkins's (1971) study of parole in New York demonstrated that importance of the inmate's appearance and demeanor at the parole hearing in determining the parole release. In addition, Piliavin and Briar (1964) found that demeanor was also of major importance in the police decision to formally process juveniles and that demeanor was very strongly correlated with race. Thus, blacks were more likely to be seen as having a "bad attitude" and consequently treated differently than whites. It is possible that a similar process may be occurring in the parole decision with Indians, being seen as having a poor presence at their parole hearing and thus being treated more harshly. Data do not presently exist to address these issues; clearly they warrant further study.

All of this has left untouched a major anomaly of these findings: If Native Americans are being so discriminated against, why do they have significantly shorter sentences? There are two possible interpretations for this phenomenon. One prevailing theory of the operation of the parole board is that is serves as the great equalizier for sentencing disparity (Stanley, 1976). That is, if two judges impose vastly different sentences for similar offenders who committed similar offenses, the parole board can serve to equalize the actual penalty that each individual will receive. There is some indication that this balancing effect occurs in the present sample between Indians and non-Indians. Multiplying the proportion of sentence served by the sentence imposed will yield a measure of total months served. Using this procedure for burglary offenders we note that Indian offenders served an average of 13.6 months while non-Indians served an average of 15.3 months. This difference is not statistically significant.

A second approach yields a different explanation for these findings. Such a situation might result if Native Americans were being sentenced to incarceration for offenses for which other defendents received less severe sanctions. In this case, it would appear consistent to argue that Indians who received a short term of incarceration were being treated more harshly than those who obtained an nonincarcerative penalty for a similar offense. Thus, what is needed to supplement the present length-of-incarceration argument is an analysis of the type of sentence. Hall and Simkus (1975) performed such an analysis and provide support for this explanation through demonstrating that Native Americans are more likely to receive an incarcerative sentence than similar white defendants.

While the findings from the present study differ from a number of studies dealing with the treatment of other racial minorities in the criminal justice system, they are consistent with other studies concerning discriminatory treatment of Native Americans. This consistently reported disparity at several decision points may suggest the existence of cumulative discrimination that should be addressed through a more comprehensive analysis of the treatment of Native American defendants at each stage of the criminal justice process.

NOTES

1. Scott's (1974) study did include race as a variable in his analysis. It, however, was not significant and was not a focal point of his investigation.

2. Hall and Simkus (1975) classified type of sentence into four categories: deferred sentence, suspended sentence, partially suspended (split sentence), and imprisonment. A gamma of .35 was reported for the relationship between being an Indian and type of sentence received.

3. In this state, good time was awarded at a rate of 2 months of good time for every 10 months of good behavior. Thus, for a one-year sentence an inmate would have to serve 10 months unless he committed prison infractions that would result in the loss of this good time. Proportion of time served was computed by calculating the actual sentence (sentence imposed minus good time) and viewing the time served as a percentage of this amount. Thus, those inmates who were released at the expiration of sentence would have a proportion of time served equal to 1.0. However, if an inmate lost good time and was released at his sentence expiration, the proportion of time served may be greater than 1.0.

4. All variables were measured continuously except race, which was coded "1" for Indians and "0" for non-Indians.

REFERENCES

Chambliss, W. and R. Seidman (1971) *Law, Order, and Power.* Reading, MA: Addison-Wesley.

Chiricos, T. P. Jackson and G. Waldo (1972) "Inequality in the imposition of a criminal label." *Social Problems* 19: 533-572.

Cole, G. (1970) "The decision to prosecute." *Law and Society Review*, 4 (February).

Dawson, R. (1966) "The decision to grant or deny parole." *Washington University Law Quarterly*, 3.

Ferdinand, T. and E. Luchterhand (170) "Inner city youth, the police, the juvenile court, and justice." *Social Problems*: 510-527.

Hagan, J. (1974) "Extra-legal attributes and Criminal sentencing: An assessment of a sociological viewpoint." *Law and Society Review* 8: 357-383.

Hall, E. and A. Simkus (1975) "Inequality in the types of sentences received by Native Americans and whites." *Criminology* 13: 199-222.

Hawkins, K. (1971) "Parole selection: The American experience." Ph.D. Dissertation, University of Cambridge.

Hepburn, J. (1978) "Race and decision to arrest: An analysis of warrants issued." *Journal of Research in Crime and Delinquency* 15: 54-73.

Hindelang, M. (1969) "Equality under the law." *Journal of Criminal Law, Criminology, and Police Science* 60: 306-313.

Packer, H. (1964) "Two models of the criminal process." *University of Pennsylvania Law Review*: 1-68.

Peterson, D. and P. Friday (1975) "Early release from incarceration: Race as a factor in the use of shock probation." *Journal of Criminal Law and Criminology*: 79-87.

Piliavin, I. and S. Briar (1964) "Police encounters with juveniles." *American Journal of Sociology* 70: 206-214.

Schur, E. (1973) *Radical Non-Intervention: Rethinking the Delinquency Problem.* Englewood Cliffs, NJ: Prentice-Hall.

Scott, J. (1974) "The use of discretion in determining the severity of punishment for incarcerated offenders." *Journal of Criminal Law and Criminology* 63: 214-224.

Stanley, D. (1976) *Prisoners Among Us: The Problem of Parole.* Washington, DC: Brookings Institution.

Swift, B. and G. Bickel (1974) *Comparative Parole Treatment of American Indians and Non-Indians at U.S. Federal Prisons.* Washington, DC: Bureau of Social Science Research.

Thornberry, T. (1973) "Race, socioeconomic status, and sentencing in the juvenile justice system." *Journal of Criminal Law and Criminology* 64: 90-98.

Turk, A. (1969) *Criminality and Legal Order.* Skokie, IL: Rand McNally.

5

RACE AND EXTREME
POLICE-CITIZEN
VIOLENCE

James J. Fyfe

The American University
The Police Foundation

The disproportionate representation of blacks among the clientele of the criminal justice system is a recurrent theme in the literature (Wolfgang, 1964: 51). Research into police firearms use (e.g., Clark, 1974: Milton et al. 1977) reports that minority disproportionality is also an explosive issue. Goldkamp (1976: 183), however, accurately notes that the present paucity of analysis of this phenomenon leaves criminal justice agencies free to adopt either of two empirically unsubstantiated "belief prespectives."
Goldkamp briefly defines those "belief perspectives" as follows:

> Some writers suggest that the disproportionately high death rate of minorities at the hands of the police can best be explained by the disproportionately high arrest rate for crimes of violence, or by assumptions concerning the suspect's responsibility for his/her own death in violent police-suspect interactions. Others see disproportionate minority deaths as resulting from both irresponsible use of deadly force by a small minority of police officers and differential administration of law enforcement toward minority citizenry (which

AUTHOR'S NOTE: This study would not have been possible had not former Chief of Operations James T. Hannon, former Chief of Personnel Neil J. Behan, former Assistant Chief Patrick S. Fitzsimons, and Lieutenant Frank McGee of the New York City Police department been so generous in providing access to the necessary data.

in effect produces disproportionately high arrest and death rates for minorities in general). Kobler and Knoohuizen, Fahey and Palmer stress the possibility that police misconduct may play a considerable role in generating civilian deaths. Takagi ascribes disproportionality to the simple fact that "police have one trigger finger for whites and another for blacks" [1976: 169].

Harding and Fahey, whose position seems to straddle both perspectives, suggest that police misconduct is involved in shooting deaths. Conversely, they also state that the use of deadly force by police "is not an independent aspect of the race problem." They write that:

> Police conduct is a dependent aspect of general patterns of criminal behavior, patterns that are significantly influenced by broader considerations of, for example, age, class, and affluence. (The) (v)ictimization of those shot is directly related to contacts of the sort in which firearms are most frequently used by criminals [1973: 310].

RACE AND EXTREME POLICE-CITIZEN VIOLENCE: TWO HYPOTHESES

Harding and Fahey suggest, therefore, that racial disproportionality among police shooting victims may be related to racial variations among other indices of violence. To some degree, this assertion is supported by the work of Kania and Mackey (1977), who found that such variations among fatal police shooting rates across the 50 states were closely related to variations in reported violent crime and criminal homicide rates. Because of our access to data on extreme police-citizen violence in New York City, these prior efforts also suggested two hypotheses which became the focus of this article.

First, on the theory that police shootings are a corollary of the frequency of contacts which present the opportunity for such violence, we postulated that:

H1: Blacks and Hispanics would be overrepresented among police shooting opponents in relation to their representation in the New

York City population but there would be less disporportion by race taking into account the racial representation of arrests for violent crime.

Second, to test the assumption that police shootings are related to other indices of extreme violence among the races:

H2: Blacks and Hispanics overrepresentation among police shooting opponents in New York City would be reduced by taking into account the racial representation in reported murders and nonnegligent manslaughters.

DATA SOURCES

Our major data source for these analyses consisted of New York City Police Department records of all incidents in which officers reported discharging weapons and/or being subject of "serious assault" (e.g., assault with deadly weapon and/or which resulted in officer death or serious injury) during the years 1971-1975. These data included "Firearms Discharge/Assault Reports" (FDAR's) filed by 4904 officers, of whom 3827 reported discharging firearms in 2926 separate "shooting incidents." Since not all these involved shooting at other human beings, we excluded from analysis such events as shootings to destroy animals, warning shots, and officer suicides. Because of the relatively low number of female opponents included in our data and because they were often involved in non-line of duty shootings (Fyfe, 1978: 145-159), we also excluded them from analysis. Conversely, because our detailed examination of the data had convinced us that the frequency of police use of firearms as a means of deadly force is best measured in terms of officer decisions to point and fire at other human beings, we included for analysis all such incidents, without regard to their consequences: with rare exception, missed shots, woundings, and fatalities are only chance variation of equally grave decisions.

While we considered this shooting data base nearly ideal for our purposes,[1] we found that available U.S. Census Bureau figures were less informative. New York City base population figures provided by the census define only two major racial groups, "White," which includes

"Mexican, Puerto Rican, or a response suggesting Indo-European stock" (U.S. Department of Commerce, 1973: B34, App7-8) and "Negro." This inclusion of Puerto Ricans and other Hispanics into the "White" category is not a major limitation insofar as measurement of shooting opponent racial disproportion is concerned, however, since New York City also develops its own population racial distributions.

More surprisingly, we also found—with one exception—that the New York City Police Department does compile racial statistics of arrestees.[2] In the absence of this ideal data source, we decided to employ two surrogate scales of comparison. For our analysis of H1, we elected to use Burnham's sample of the races of 700 persons arrested for murder, nonnegligent manslaughter, robbery, forcible rape, and felonious assault in New York City (1973: 50).[3] Because we were similarly precluded from using homicide arrestee data in our examination of H2, we decided to employ information on the race of homicide victims. Here, since many studies show that homicides tend to be intraracial crimes, it might not be unreasonable to consider the victim index as a crude proxy for the perpetrator index.

H1: ANALYSIS

Given these limitations, our data do indicate that Blacks and Hispanics are disporportionately represented among those New York City police shooting opponents whose race is recorded. Table 1 demonstrates that Whites, who comprise 64.1% of New York City's population total, represent only 17.5% of its shooting opponents. Blacks, conversely, are overrepresented among shooting opponents in almost exactly the reverse ratio: 60.2% of shooting opponents and 20.5% of total city population are Black. Hispanics, who number 15.4% of city population, represent 22.3% of shooting opponents.

Using the racial composition of the general population of the city as expected frequencies, we derived a chi-square for these distributions which is significant at the .001 level. Similarly, our obtained Cramer's v (.49)[4] suggests a rather high association between race and the likelihood of being shot at by New York City police. The first part of this hypothesis is therefore confirmed.

Turning now to a model (Table 2) which utilized the ethnic distribution of felony arrests for violent crimes (Burnham's data) to generate expected

TABLE 1   Racial Distribution of New York City Police
           Shooting Opponents, and New York City
           Population January 1, 1971-December 31, 1975

	Shooting Opponents[a]		*New York City Population*	
White	17.5%	(549)	64.1%	(5076022)
Black	60.2%	(1889)	20.5%	(1621583)
Hispanic	22.3%	(701)	15.4%	(1216557)
TOTALS	100.0%	(3139)	100.0%	(7914162)

chi-square = 1488.40

p = .001

v = .49

[a]Excludes "Other" racial categories because of low statistical significance.
Ten shooting opponents were identified as members of "Other" racial
groups.

[b]Calculated from: New York City Police Department, Chief of Field
Services, *Summary of Precinct Populations, 1973.*

TABLE 2   Racial Distribution of New York City Police
           Shooting Opponents, and Persons Arrested
           For Felonies Against the Person January 1,
           1971-December 31, 1975

	Shooting Opponents	*Felony Arrests*[a]
White	17.5%	22.2%
Black	60.2%	62.4%
Hispanic	22.3%	15.4%
TOTALS	100.0%	100.0%

chi-square = 12.82

p= .01

v = .09

[a] Calculated from a sample of 700 persons arrested for murder, nonnegligent manslaughter, robbery, felonious assault and forcible
rape in New York City, 1971. Source: David Burnham, "3 of 5
Slain by Police Here are Black, Same as Arrest Rate," *The New York
Times*, August 26, 1973, 50.

TABLE 3   Racial Distribution of New York City Police
Shooting Opponents, January 1, 1971-December
31, 1975 and Victims of Murder and Non-Negligent
Manslaughter,[a] January 1, 1971-December 31, 1975

	Shooting Opponents	Homicide Victims
White	17.5% (549)	22.5% (1069)
Black	60.2% (1889)	51.0% (2419)
Hispanic	22.3% (701)	26.5% (1259)
Totals	100.0% (3139)	100.0% (4747)

chi-square = 54.68
p = .001
v = .09

[a] Source: New York City Police Department, Homicide Analysis Unit,
        Annaul Report, 1976

numbers of shooting opponents by ethnicity, it may be seen that there   is
a fairly close fit. Although the chi-square is still significant, the v value is
now only .09, or much smaller   ha   the v value of .49 reported for Table
1. While Whites rCemaiin slightly underrepresented among shooting
opponents, Blacks are also underrepresented. Only Hispanics are overrepresented. Some caution must be observed about the finer distinctions in view
of the limitations of data on ethnic classifications.

H2: ANALYSIS

Using our murder and nonnegligent manslaughter victim racial distributions to generate expected frequencies of shooting opponents by race
(Table 3), we find that there is a fairly close fit. Again Cramer's v is only
.09, which suggests that there is a close parallel between the racial
distributions of homicide victims and police shooting opponents.

TABLE 4   Age Characteristics of New York City Male
Population by Ethnic Group

	Black	Puerto Rican	White
Median Male Age	23.1	19.4	33.3
Percentage of Male Population Under 18	42.0	45.6	27.6

SOURCE: U.S. Department of Commerce. *Characteristics of the Population*, Part 34 NY Section 1, March 1973 U.S. Government Printing Office, pp. 34-108, 34-432.

FURTHER COMMENTS

Even if both the relationships shown in Tables 2 and 3 were demonstrated by more comprehensive arrest and victim data, they would not prove that the disproportionate involvement of Blacks and Hispanics in shooting incidents is related to their disproportionate involvement as violent crime arrestees and homicide victims.

Most specifically, we would still be left with the possibility that both relationships are spurious and merely reflections of varying degrees of risk due to differential age distributions and/or differential enforcement and police deployment practices. It is still possible that the races are differentially represented among shooting opponents because more Blacks and Hispanics fall into the age groups most frequently involved in these incidents. Alternatively, it is still possible that Blacks and Hispanics are disproportionately represented among shooting opponents because police do have "one trigger finger for Whites and another for minorities." Table 4, which summarized the age characteristics of New York City's male Whites, Blacks, and Puerto Ricans (the city's major Hispanic subpopulation), confirms the existence of differential age distributions among these groups. As Table 4 indicates, New York City's white males are generally considerably older (median age = 33.3 years) than either its male blacks (median age = 23.1 years) or its male Puerto Ricans (median age = 19.4 years).

To determine whether similar age discrepancies existed among the shooting opponents included in our data, we crosstabulated opponent race

TABLE 5   New York City Police Shooting Incident Opponent Race by Age, January 1, 1971-December 31, 1975

Opponent	Under 16	16, 17	18, 19	20, 21	22, 23	24, 25	26, 27	28, 29	30+	Totals
					Opponent Age					
White	3.2% (13)	10.6% (43)	15.0% (62)	14.5% (59)	10.6% (43)	11.3% (46)	4.9% (20)	7.2% (29)	22.7% (92)	18.9% (407)
Black	3.6% (44)	8.7% (107)	12.8% (185)	13.7% (169)	12.5% (155)	12.7% (158)	7.5% (93)	5.8% (72)	22.7% (280)	57.6% (1236)
Hispanic	2.0% (10)	11.1% (56)	10.5% (53)	13.1% (66)	10.7% (54)	11.1% (56)	7.9% (40)	5.9% (30)	27.7% (140)	23.5% (505)
Totals	3.1% (67)	9.6% (206)	12.7% (273)	13.7% (294)	11.7% (252)	12.1% (260)	7.1% (153)	6.1% (131)	23.9% (512)	100.0% (2148)

chi-square = 3.866
p = .99
v = .03

TABLE 6   New York City Male Shooting Opponent Race
Per 10,000 Population, by Age and Race,[a]
January 1, 1971-December 31, 1975

Age	White/Hispanic	Black
15-19	10.04	38.82
20-24	11.40	67.38
25-29	7.62	43.06
30-34	6.02	21.92
35-39	3.88	15.02
40-44	1.77	9.24
45-49	.98	4.54
50+	.16	1.86
Totals	3.95	24.20

[a] Excludes opponents under fifteen years of age (White/Hispanic
n=9; Black n=17).

and age. The results of this analysis are presented in Table 5 and demonstrate that the age distributions of shooting opponents vary little among races, a finding that runs counter to those of Jenkins and Faison (1974) and Kobler (1975). Indeed, our obtained levels of p (.99) and v (.03) indicate that these three age distributions are so close as to be nearly indistinguishable.

Table 5 also suggests that confrontation with armed police is largely an activity of the young.[5] More than half (1093) of the 2149 opponents whose race and age are included in our data set are less than 24 years old. Older opponents are not entirely excluded, however, since almost one-quarter (23.9%) of the group are 30 or more years old.[6]

Table 6 presents the frequency of shooting opponents per 10,000 population aggregated by Census Bureau age and race subgroups. Examination of Table 6 reveals that White/Hispanic and Black age distributions are very similar. For both race groupings, those 20 to 24 years old are most frequently involved in shootings; subsequently the rates steadily decline for each age subgroup, reaching the lowest levels among those 50 or more years old. The only major discrepancy in age trends occurs for the 15-to-19-year age group; the White/Hispanic male rate is only slightly less than that of the 20-to-24-year group, while for Blacks the rate of 15-to-19-year-olds is substantially lower than for 20-to-24-year-olds.

Equally as striking as the general similarities in age patterns are the great numeric discrepancies in rates. Specifically, we find that Black males are six times more likely to have been involved in police shooting incidents (24.20 per 10,000 population) than are male White/Hispanics (3.95 per 10,000). Indeed, the overall Black male rate (24.20) is more than twice as large as the highest White/Hispanic male rate (11.40). The general discrepancy ratio holds in each and every age group and is strongest within the 20-29 year range.

RACIAL DISPROPORTION

To this point, our investigation has shown that the variable of race is linked to the likelihood of being a police shooting opponent; in a similar fashion, this risk factor is apparently linked to arrest rates for violent felonies. The possibility remains that the great numeric disproportion of minorities among both arrestees and shooting opponents is a function of differential police enforcement or deployment practices.

Since most prior literature which addresses racial disproportion among opponents (e.g., Goldkamp, 1976; Harding and Fahey, 1973; Robin, 1963; Jenkins and Faison, 1974) examines only fatal shootings, we commenced our investigation with an analysis of incident consequences in terms of opponent injury. Table 7 provides a crosstabulation of reported shooting opponent race by injury and demonstrates that these consequences vary little among the races. Regardless of race, approximately 3 in 5 opponents suffer no injury, 1 in 5 is wounded, 1 in 10 is killed, and 1 in 10 escapes after the police have shot at him with unknown effect. Once an officer decides to employ his "trigger finger," the race of his opponent apparently matters little in terms of the effect of police shots. Blacks escape with unknown injuries approximately twice as often (16.6%) as Whites (7.9%) or Hispanics (9.8%), but as our obtained chi-square (p = .50) indicates that even this variance is likely to be a result of chance.

This lack of variance "within" confrontations, obviously, does not address numeric disproportionality. Stated most simply, we can observe little difference among the races once they become involved in conflict situations: We have not, however, touched on the issue of why so many minority opponents become involved in these incidents in the first instance.

TABLE 7   New York City Police Shooting Opponent Race by
Injury January 1, 1971-December 31, 1975[a]

Opponent Race	Opponent Injury				
	None	Wounded	Killed	Unknown[b]	Totals
White	61.8%	21.0%	9.2%	7.9%	17.6%
	(335)	(114)	(50)	(43)	(542)
Black	53.4%	21.0%	9.1%	16.6%	60.0%
	(983)	(386)	(168)	(305)	(1842)
Hispanic	56.0%	22.2%	12.1%	9.8%	22.3%
	(384)	(152)	(83)	(67)	(686)
Totals	55.4%	21.2%	9.8%	13.5%	100.0% [c]
	(1702)	(652)	(301)	(415)	(3072)

chi-square = 5.45

p = .50

v = .03

[a]Excludes cases in which opponent race not reported; excludes 4 suicides
(1 White, 2 Black, 1 Hispanic).

[b]Not apprehended opponents at whom shots were fired with unknown
effect.

[c]Percentage subcells may not total 100.0 due to rounding.

To examine this question, we attempted to determine whether there
existed significant variation among the types of shooting incidents in
which different races became involved. We hypothesized that if we found
high frequencies of incidents in which police shot at unarmed Blacks or
Hispanics, it would suggest that police did, indeed, have "different trigger
fingers" for minorities. Conversely, we felt that significant differences
among the races in the precipitating event types and the degree of danger
confronting police might help to explain the disproportion of minority
opponents.

To simplify this process and clarify its results, we decided to employ
the race of each incident's "primary opponent."[7] This resulted in very
little loss of accuracy since incidents involving multiple opponents are
overwhelmingly intraracial events.[8] Further, since our operative definition
of "primary opponent" translated into either the only opponent or the
one posing the greatest threat to police (e.g., the most combative, most

heavily armed), we concluded that it was this person's conduct upon which police reaction (or overreaction) would be principally based. Thus, a shooting precipitated by a robbery involving one Black suspect armed with a gun and a White one armed with a knife becomes a "Black opponent" incident.

Our first measure of variance in shooting incident types among the races involved an investigation of the events which precipitated police shooting. As Table 8 and its chi-square significance level (.00001) reveal, there is considerable variance here. Perhaps most striking is the great frequency with which police confront Blacks at robberies. Indeed, nearly half (45.8%) of the incidents involving Blacks were reportedly initiated by robberies. This is a rate nearly twice that of Whites and Hispanics (23.4% and 26.3%, respectively) and represents a raw frequency (495 incidents) greater than the total of all incidents involving either Whites (354) or Hispanics (429). We see, in fact, that robberies involving Black primary opponents comprise 26.6% of all the incidents included in Table 8.

Table 8 also demonstrates that Whites are disproportionately more frequently counted among those who confront police at burglaries (12.4% versus 6.4% and 9.1% for Blacks and Hispanics, respectively). In addition, perhaps because of the general relationship between race and social status, the percentages of "Car Stop" incidents involving Blacks (11.3%) and Hispanics (8.4%) are far smaller than those of Whites (19.5%). Similarly, the percentage of "Other" incidents, which often include offduty disputes and the like, is greater for Whites (10.5%) and Hispanics (9.3%) than for Blacks (4.0%). Conversely, Whites are less frequently involved in generally proactive "Investigative Suspicious Person"—or "Stop and Question"— incidents than are Blacks and Hispanics (7.3% versus 11.0% and 16.6%, respectively). Finally, Table 8 reveals considerable difference in the frequencies of "Respond to Disturbance" incidents: 15.6% for Hispanics, 10.2% for Whites, and 9.0% for Blacks.

A measure of the threat of officer safety at these incidents is provided by Table 9, which crosstabulates primary-opponent race with weapon type. Here again, it can be seen that striking differences exist among the races, with the chi-square proving significant to .0001. Approximately half of Black and Hispanic opponents (52.9%) and 48.0%) were armed with handguns. Nearly half (47.2%) of all incidents included in Table 9 were police confrontations with Hispanic or Blacks armed with handguns, rifles, machine guns, or shotguns; White handgun, rifle, machine gun, or shotgun incidents account for 6.9% of all incidents. Conversely, we find that Whites are more frequently involved in incidents involving no weapon

TABLE 8 New York City Police Shooting Primary Opponent Race by Precipitating Event, January 1, 1971-December 31, 1975

Primary Opponent Race	Respond to Disturbance	Burglary	Robbery	Attempt other Arrests	Handling Prisoner	Investigating Suspicious Persons	Ambush	Mentally Deranged	Auto Pursuit/ Stop	Assault on Officer	Other	Totals
White	10.2% (36)	12.4% (44)	23.4% (83)	4.2% (15)	0.8% (3)	7.3% (26)	0.3% (1)	2.5% (9)	19.5% (69)	8.8% (31)	10.5% (37)	19.0% (354)
Black	9.0% (97)	6.4% (69)	45.8% (495)	3.1% (34)	1.6% (17)	11.0% (119)	0.9% (10)	1.5% (16)	11.3% (122)	5.4% (58)	4.0% (43)	58.0% (1080)
Hispanic	15.6% (67)	9.1% (39)	26.3% (113)	4.9% (21)	1.2% (5)	16.6% (71)	0.9% (4)	2.1% (9)	8.4% (36)	5.6% (24)	9.3% (40)	23.0% (429)
Totals	10.7% (200)	8.2% (152)	37.1% (691)	3.8% (70)	1.3% (25)	11.6% (216)	0.8% (15)	1.8% (34)	12.2% (227)	6.1% (113)	6.4% (120)	100.0% (1863)

Not ascertained = 15

Chi-square = 151.88078

p = .00001

v = .20

TABLE 9   New York City Police Shooting Primary Opponent Race by Weapon, January 1, 1971-December 31, 1975

Primary Opponent Race		Type of Weapon							
	None	Handgun	Rifle/ Machine Gun	Shotgun	Knife/ Cutting Instrument	Vehicle	Physical Force	Other	Total
White	15.5% (56)	32.1% (116)	1.4% (5)	1.9% (7)	13.3% (48)	16.1% (58)	9.4% (34)	10.2% (37)	19.2% (361)
Black	7.8% (85)	52.9% (574)	1.3% (14)	6.3% (68)	14.1% (153)	6.1% (66)	4.2% (46)	7.4% (80)	57.8% (1086)
Hispanic	5.1% (22)	48.0% (207)	2.6% (11)	3.1% (14)	21.3% (92)	6.3% (27)	5.1% (22)	8.4% (36)	22.9% (431)
Totals	8.7% (163)	47.8% (897)	1.6% (30)	4.7% (89)	15.6% (293)	8.0% (151)	5.4% (102)	8.1% (153)	100.0% [a] (1878)

chi-square = 131.62032

p = .00001

v = .19

[a]Subcell percentages may not total 100.0 due to rounding

TABLE 10 New York City Police Firearms Discharge/Assault Incident Primary Opponent Race by Officer Injury,[a] January 1, 1971-December 31, 1975

Primary Opponent Race	Officer Injury			
	None	*Injured*	*Killed*	*Totals*
White	76.4% (402)	22.8% (120)	.8% (4)	17.5% (526)
Black	82.2% (1471)	16.6% (297)	1.2% (21)	59.6% (1789)
Hispanic	81.3% (557)	18.0% (123)	.7% (5)	22.8% (685)
Totals	81.0% (2430)	18.0% (540)	1.0% (30)	100.0% [b] (3000)

chi-square = 1.84

p = .80

v = .02

[a]Includes only officers wounded or killed in the line of duty.

[b]Subcell percentages may not total 100.0 due to rounding.

or no assault on police (15.5%) than are Blacks (7.8%) or Hispanics (5.1%). Whites are also overrepresented in incidents involving the use of vehicles (16.1% versus 6.1% for Blacks, 6.3% for Hispanics) or physical force (9.4% versus 4.2% and 5.1%) as means of assaulting police. Hispanics use knives against police considerably more often (21.3%) than do Whites (13.3%) or Blacks (14.1%). Given that most police are killed or seriously injured by guns or knife wounds, therefore, we would tentatively conclude that Blacks and Hispanics are more often involved—both proportionately and in terms of sheer numbers—in incidents that present greater potential danger to police than are Whites.

That potential danger does not necessarily translate into real negative consequences in terms of officer injury is indicated by Table 10, which provides a crosstabulation of FDAR incident primary-opponent race by degree of officer injury (excluding non-line of duty injuries, which are not relevant to this analysis). Here, although the nature and seriousness of nonfatal injuries are not specified and, in fact, vary considerably, it can be seen that proportionately more officers are injured in encounters with

Whites (22.8%) or Hispanics (18.0%). Proportionately more officers are killed in the line-of-duty by Blacks (1.2%) than by Whites (.8%) or by Hispanics (.7%).[9] Although Table 10's chi-square indicates that differences among these distributions are not significant (p = .80), it is also important to note that 55% of line-of-duty officer injuries and deaths occur with Black opponents.

SOME CONCLUSIONS

In summarizing this research within the context of prior literature and the limits of our data, we are led to two major conclusions. First, Harding and Fahey's assertion that minority disproportion among police shooting opponents is related to differential age distributions among the races is, in New York City at least, inaccurate. Our data demonstrate that, while police shooting opponents are generally young and a greater proportion of the Black population is young, Black males in all age groups are considerably more liable to become police shooting opponents than are their White/Hispanics contemporaries.

Our second conclusion deals with whether that greater liability is associated with greater Black participation in activities most likely to lead to justifiable extreme police-citizen violence or with "the simple fact the 'police have one trigger finger for whites and another for blacks.'" Here we are led to choose Goldkamp's "Belief Perspective II": Our data indicate that Blacks make up a disproportionate share of shooting opponents reportedly armed with guns and a disproprotionate share of those reportedly engaged in robberies when police intervened. If one accepts both the accuracy of these reports and the premise that opponents armed with guns generally present the greatest and most immediate danger to police, there is little to support the contention that Blacks are shot disproportionately in relatively trivial and nonthreatening situations. A more conclusive answer to the question would require the calculation of shooting rates for specific arrest situations by race. As was indicated earlier, the lack of race information on arrests precludes this analysis.

Although our research has not conclusively confirmed Goldkamp's Belief Perspective II, it has reduced to two the assumptions upon which one might base acceptance of the "police misconduct" and "different trigger finger" hypotheses implicit in his alternate theory. First, of course, one might not accept the accuracy of the reports of Black/gun incidents which account for most of our data set's Black opponent disproportion. The sheer number of those shootings (656 are shown on Table 9), however, is so large as to suggest that the argument that "irresponsible use of deadly force by a small number of police officers" accounts for disproportionate minority deaths is ill-founded.

Second, one might accept the accuracy of these reports, but properly note that we have not demonstrated that New York police do not refrain from shooting at Whites in situations comparable to those in which they do shoot at Blacks. Since most of the Black opponents in our data set were reportedly armed with guns, the assumption based on this observation requires its proponents to argue that police generally regard Blacks with guns as more threatening than Whites with guns. Our own logic and experience, however, suggest that police responses to such situations are based not upon opponent race, but rather upon opponent weapon.

Finally, we must qualify our acceptance of Goldkamp's Belief Perspective II. There is nothing in these analyses to support the contention that the disproportion of Blacks among New York City police shooting opponents is reflective of police misconduct or racial discrimination; but the limitations of our data have prevented us from examining the degree to which that disproportion is associated with the generally lower socioeconomic position of Blacks. Differences among the shooting types which characterize the races (e.g., the high incidence of Black participation in shootings precipitated by robberies, which are most frequent in blighted inner city areas and the high incidence of shootings involving Whites and vehicles, often preceded by car thefts, which are most frequently in middle and working class areas), however, suggest that this association may be strong.

Were we to conduct further research based upon data which included information about opponent socioeconomic status, we would hypothesize that Harding and Fahey's assessment of the role of class and affluence in shooting opponent racial disproportion would be confirmed. Were we successful, our research would strongly indicate that Black shooting opponent disproportion is neither a consequence of "overreaction" by individual police officers nor of some racially varying predispositions toward violent crime. Conversely, it would point up the continuing existence of *An American Dilemma* described so well by Myrdal (1944) a generation ago; Blacks are the mode among New York's police shooting opponents because they are also the mode among the lower socioeconomic groups which most frequently participate in the types of activity likely to precipitate extreme police-citizen violence.

NOTES

1. Our reservations here involve the accuracy and degree of detail provided in the shooting incident reports filed by individual officers. Because we attempted to limit our analyses to variables reasonably immune to reporting bias (and often supported by witness statements), we regarded the question of the veracity of the data we did possess as one of minor importance. We were more troubled by the impact on our research of the data we did not possess: 1058 (25.1%) of the data set's shooting opponents were not identified by race. We did not find any evidence that this information was deliberately withheld from reports in order to prevent or avoid any sensitive racial issues. This is so for several reasons. First, the "Firearms Discharge/ Assault Report" forms which served as our primary data source include no caption requesting "opponent race," so that it appears only on reports filed by officers who volunteered it. These forms, originally designed to collect information for training purposes, have more recently been supplemented by more complete narrative reports. As a result, the annual percentage of missing opponent race data declined from nearly 40% in 1971 to 5.4% in 1975. Second, despite this regular decrease in missing data, annual known opponent racial distributions have remained relatively constant over the period studied. Third, the percentage of missing opponent race data is relatively evenly distributed across the city's police precincts, regardless of the racial character- istics of their total populations (which one might reasonably expect to impact upon the characteristics of their shooting opponents). Fourth, our opponent data suggests that many of these opponents were never seen by the officers involved: More than 9 of 10 "unknowns" (90.6%) suffered no injury (72.6%) or escaped their confrontation with unknown injuries (18.0%). Further, our opponent arrest data reveal that 397 (37.5%) of opponents whose race is classified as unknown were not apprehended by police: In many cases, these individuals were merely shadowy figures encountered on dimly lit streets or rooftops.

2. Except for homicides, the department began compiling these statistics only in 1976. The department's Homicide Analysis Section began systematically recording the race of those arrested for homicide in 1973. We elected not to use these data in our analyses because they do not describe the experience for the full five years of our study and because they do not identify homicide perpetrators who are not appre- hended.

3. Burnham's sample is not random, but consists of 700 consecutive arrestees.

4. See Loether and McTavish who describe Cramer's v as follows:

Cramer's v is, so to speak, a properly normed measure of association for bivariat distributions of nominal variables, it is "margin free" in that the number or distribution of cases in row or column totals does not influence its value, nor is it influenced by the number of categories of either variable . . . Cramer's v . . . can only be thought of as a magnitude on a scale between zero and 1.0; the bigger the number, the stronger the association. It can *not* be interpreted, for example, as the percentage of variation in one variable explained by the other, nor can it be interpreted as the proportions of predictive error which may be reduced by prior knowledge of one of the variables [1974: 197-198].

5. By aggregating our opponent age data into eight values to conform with those reported on New York City Police arrest data, we also found that the age distributions of shooting opponents and violent felony arrestees closely parralleled each other (v = .09).

6. The decision to create this open-ended age grouping (which includes individuals up to 79 years old) was made to simplify presentation and discussion of opponent age. The frequencies of single-year values drop off dramatically after this point.

7. We defined the "primary opponent" as the only opponent or, in incidents involving more than one opponent, as the most heavily armed and/or most aggressive and/or most seriously injured.

8. Intraracial events accounted for 94.4% of the multiple-opponent shootings in which opponent race was reported.

9. These differences would shrink if four alleged politically motivated "Black Liberation Army" assassinations were considered apart from other officer deaths perpetrated by Blacks.

REFERENCES

Breasted, M. (1974) "Police use cars and clubs to quell Brownsville Riot." *New York Times* (September 20): 20.

Burnham, D. (1973) "3 of 5 slain by police here are Black, same as the arrest rate." *New York Times* (August 26): 20.

Clark, K. (1974) *Open Letter to Mayor Abraham D. Beame and Police Commissioner Michael J. Codd.* New York, September 17, 1974.

Fyfe, J. J. (1978) "Shots fired: An examination of New York City Police firearms discharges." Ph.D. dissertation, State University of New York at Albany.

Goldkamp, J. S. (1976) "Minorities as victims of police shooting: Interpretations of racial disproportionality and police use of deadly force." *Justice System Journal*, 2: 169-183.

Harding, R.W. and R.P. Fahey (1973) "Killings by Chicago police, 1969-70: An empirical study." *Southern California Law Review*, 4: 284-315.

Jenkins, B. and A. Faison (1974) *An Analysis of 248 Persons Killed by New York City Policemen.* New York: Metropolitan Applied Research Center.

Kania, R.R.E. and W. C. Mackey (1977) "Police violence as a function of community characteristics." *Criminology*, 15: 27-48.

Kobler, A. L. "Police homicide in a democracy" *Journal of Social Issues*, 31: 163-184.

Loether, H. J. and D. G. McTavish. *Descriptive Statistics For Sociologists.* Boston: Allyn and Bacon.

Milton, C. H., J. W. Halleck; J. Lardner, and G. L. Abrecht (1977) *Police Use of Deadly Force*, Washington, DC: Police Foundation.

Myrdal, G. (1944) *An American Dilemma: The Negro Problem and Modern Democracy.* New York: Harper & Row.

New York City Police Department (1976) *Annual Report*. New York: Homicide Analysis Unit.

––– (1973) *Summary of Precinct Populations*. New York: Chief of Field Services.

––– (1971-1975) *Monthly Arrest Report*. New York: Crime Analysis Unit.

New York State Penal Law (1967) Albany: New York State Government.

Robin, G. D. (1963) "Justifiable homicide by police officers." *Journal of Criminal Law, Criminology and Police Science*, 225-231.

U.S. Department of Commerce (1973) *Characteristics of the Population*. Washington, DC: Government Printing Office.

Wolfgang, M. (1958) *Patterns in Criminal Homicide*. Philadelphia: University of Pennsylvania Press.

6

BLACK AND WHITE VIOLENT DELINQUENTS: A Longitudinal Cohort Study

Richard L. Schuster

Virginia Polytechnic Institute and State University

INTRODUCTION

Black Overrepresentation

The controversy over the correlation between race and criminal involvement is as old as the discipline of criminology. No current writer would support the proposition that crime is racially determined. However, official crime reports such as the Federal Bureau of Investigation's (FBI) Uniform Crime Report and studies using official statistics consistently report black crime rates which are much higher than the proportion of blacks in the population (e.g., Forsland, 1966; Mulvihill and Tumin, 1969; Wolfgang et al., 1972; Kelley, 1975). More significantly, black overrepresentation is much higher for violent crimes than for property offenses. Nationally, nearly half (47.1%) of those arrested for FBI Index violent arrests but less than a third (29.6%) of the Index property arrests were black (Kelley, 1975: 192). While no one would seriously argue that racial characteristics cause crime, the consistency of the crime statistics, especially in regard to violent crime, has kept the issue of a correlation between race and crime current and troubling.

Many writers have argued that official statistics distort the "real" involvement of blacks in crime and have turned to self-report surveys as an alternative. Generally these studies report equal amounts of crime for blacks and whites (Chambliss and Nagasawa, 1969; Hirshi, 1969; Gould, 1969; Tracy, 1978). A few projects indicate that black youths reported more offenses or more of the serious offenses than white youths (Illinois Institute for Juvenile Research, 1972; Williams and Gold, 1972; Gold and Reiss, 1974). The majority of these studies challenge the assumption of black overrepresentation in crime though they are far from conclusive. A major problem with self-report studies is that unless stratified sampling is used, the number of black youths sampled is small. Few of these studies have specifically focused on racial differences (Pope, 1978: 351).

Other writers have attempted to explain black overrepresentation in crime statistics as a function of differential handling by police, court personnel, and judges. Many studies have examined the relationship between race and differentials in legal decision making for juveniles.[1] Most studies show that blacks are significantly more likely to be arrested, referred for court hearings, and/or institutionalized than whites. These studies document the fact that blacks are not only overrepresented in arrest statistics but also at every stage in the juvenile justice system. Some of these studies show that police are more likely to arrest blacks and courts deal more harshly with blacks even for crimes of comparable seriousness (Goldman, 1963; Ferdinand and Luchterhand, 1970; Thornberry, 1973). However, a number of researchers report that if offense seriousness, prior arrests, and/or other factors are held constant, racial bias does not seem to be an important factor (Eaton and Polk, 1961; Shannon, 1963; Terry, 1967; Hohenstein, 1969; Black and Reiss, 1970). Conclusions from these studies support the existence of differential handling of blacks but are inconclusive as to whether the differences are the function of racial prejudice. Neither the self-report surveys nor the studies of decision making have dispelled the controversy surrounding the connection between race and crime. Until much more research is done, this controversy will continue to rage.

Violence as a Crucial Issue

The need to study violent offenses and offenders, especially violent juvenile offenders, is crucial because public sentiment and fear has brought a demand for action (Levitch and Vlock, 1971: 24). Public officials have responded with numerous "reforms," many of which have been aimed at reshaping the juvenile justice system (Schuster, 1978: 9-10). Unfortunately, these actions have been based on very little empirical knowledge. While more research is now being done, there is still much to learn about violent youths.[2] As Vera noted:

> Despite the abundance of research on delinquency, data on the incidence of violence among the delinquent population and the characteristics of violent delinquents must be pieced together from a variety of sources, leaving gaps that can be filled only by guesswork [1976: 255].

It is important to gather basic information concerning the incidence and characteristics of violence and violent juvenile offenders. This need for information is especially pertinent when applied to the question of racial differences and juvenile violence. As noted earlier, blacks are arrested for about half of the violent Index offenses. Black youths (under 18 years) are overrepresented even more with 52.4% of these arrests in their age group compared to 45.5% of the violent arrests by blacks in the "18 years and over" group. Further, a strong relationship between violent (injury) crime and race was described in the influential Wolfgang et al. (1972) juvenile cohort study. In short, the disproportionately high number of black juveniles in the arrests statistics dictates a need for further research into this area.

While the connection between race and violent crime is an important topic for study, very little of the literature in criminology addresses this topic. Wolfgang's (1958) study of murder in Philadelphia and a recent work by Heilbrun and Heilbrun (1977) are the exceptions. The self-report studies are of little help in this question because they tap so few serious violent offenders. The well-known and much-used Short and Nye Scale (Short and Nye, 1958: 298) only asks for such minor actions as fist fighting, unarmed robbery (strong-arm), gang fighting, "beating up" kids, or hurting someone to see him squirm. Such crimes as murder, manslaughter, aggravated assault, rape, or armed robbery are rarely discovered in self-report studies let alone systematically examined.

The relationship between race and crime, especially violent crime, continues to be a controversial one. There is a crucial need for research on this issue. This study contributes to the literature by presenting data from a longitudinal cohort study of black and white youths arrested for violent offenses. Longitudinal cohort studies are needed to measure the extent of a phenomenon in a given population (Wolfgang et al., 1972: 7-9). Erickson documents the need for such studies when he states:

Although the desirability of interpreting delinquency and crime of cohorts has been recognized for a long time, longitudinal and panel studies are notably absent from the literature. Questions concerning patterns of career delinquency, maturational reform, the preventative and/or labeling effects of differential official reactions and processing techniques are probably only resolvable with longitudinal data. The use of a birth cohort is one method of providing much needed evidence on these aspects of delinquency [1972: 362].

This descriptive study determines the incidence of official violent involvement for a specific population and examines the social and arrest characteristics of violent juveniles from that population. Social variables include race, socioeconomic status, family composition, and companionate crime. Arrest variables include total number of arrests, age of onset, spacing between violent arrests, type of arrest offense, and disposition of arrest. The dynamic nature of the arrest career is examined, using age of onset, spacing, and the position of violent arrests.

METHODOLOGY

The population of violent juveniles for this study consists of *all* youths born in the years 1956 through 1960 who were arrested by the Columbus City Police for at least one violent offense. Violent offenses in this study include murder, manslaughter, rape, sexual battery, robbery (armed and unarmed), assault (simple and aggravated), sexual imposition, and molesting. A civilian employee of the Columbus City Police searched all juvenile records from 1956 on and when she encountered a record for a youth who fit these criteria, his/her entire delinquent arrest file was removed, copied, and then forwarded to the project office.

A total of 1,162 youths were selected in this manner, but 24 were removed because they were not Franklin County residents. This left 1,138 youths for the study but those born in 1959 and 1960 had not yet completed their juvenile careers. To prevent distortion of the findings, only the 811 youths who had "maxed out" (i.e., completed their juvenile careers) were used for the portions of this analysis devoted to "career" analysis.

For those youths who were committed to the Ohio Youth Commission, the dates of all commitments and releases were obtained and coded. These dates were used to determine the "street time" spacing variables and to learn how much "time" had been served by youths in this study.

Two limitations of the study must be mentioned. First, verification of the presence of all of these youths in Franklin County for their entire juvenile career was not possible. Migration, death (in one known case), and undetected lengthy incarcerations are factors that must be recognized as limitations on the completeness of the data. Second, the use of arrest statistics to represent delinquent involvement has obvious drawbacks. Racial differences may be a function of prejudicial handling or real differences in the populations. However, finding a sizable population of violent juveniles through other methods such as self-reports involves other significant problems. Both of these problems mean that these data represent only minimum estimates of involvement.

FINDINGS

Franklin County and its Violent Population

In 1975 Columbus, Ohio, had an estimated population of 536,000 which ranked 22nd in the United States. The Standard Metropolitan Statistical Area population totaled 1,069,000, the 35th among the statistical areas (U.S. Bureau of the Census, 1975). The official violent crime problem in Columbus, and Franklin County, was not as serious as other comparable cities.[3] In 1976 the *Uniform Crime Report* rate of violent crime was 438.5 per 100,000 inhabitants, which is close to the national average of 460 but far below the 1,095.4 average rate for cities with populations exceeding 250,000 (Kelley, 1977: 57,153). Thus the Columbus violent population may differ somewhat from violent populations in other cities.

In 1970 the 1956-1960 birth cohort totaled 84,792 youths; the 1956-1958 age group was estimated at 50,875 (U.S. Bureau of the Census, 1970). From this latter cohort a total of 811 youths were arrested at least once for violent offenses. While Franklin County was 12.5% black (Columbus was 18.5% black), slightly over half (54.8% or 442 youths) of the violent 1956-1958 cohort was black and 45.3% (367 youths) was white.[4] This percent of blacks is remarkably similar to the arrest proportions cited by Liska and Tausig (1979: 199) for three other very dissimilar delinquent populations—Thornberry (1973) found that 55.8% of his arrest sample was black; Arnold (1974) reported 56.3% and Ferdinand and Luchterhand (1970) showed 57.5%. No explanation for this striking similarity can be provided.

Violent white youths made up .85% of the 1956-1958 white cohort while violent black youths constituted 5.64% of theirs. Violent white males represent 1.5% of the white male cohort; violent black males 9.1% of theirs.

Blacks, especially black males, are greatly overrepresented in these statistics. Black males constituted only about 8% of the Franklin County 1956-1958 cohort, but accounted for 43.8% of the violent cohort. It should be noted, however, that while the total number of "actual" violent juveniles can never be known, those that come into contact with the justice system, black or white, comprise a very small segment of the juvenile population as a whole. Black males, the most overrepresented group, represent less than a tenth of their cohort.

Socioeconomic status (SES) was derived by determining the census tract of each youth and using the median income of that tract to represent the youth's SES.[5] All youths in tracts below the Franklin County median income were designated as "Lower SES" (see Wolfgang et al., 1972). The vast majority (85.9%) of the violent youths fell into this category. Blacks were much more likely to be Lower SES (94.8%) than whites (75.2%; Cramer's V = .278). The "Lower SES" category was further subdivided along Housing and Urban Development (HUD) guidelines which designate 20% and 80% of median income as further cutpoints for classification. Those with 20% and below were labelled "very poor," 21% to 80% were "poor," 81% to median income were "moderate." No white youths were from "very poor" tracts, though 11.3% of the black youths were. Given the skewed nature of the whole violent population (i.e., only 14% came from tracts above median income), the relationship between SES and race was remarkably high (Cramer's V = .348 for the four-class HUD distribution). Race and SES were intercorrelated, such that SES may also explain differential selection into a violent delinquent population.

Males of both races dominated the statistics. Only a tenth (10.6%) of the whites and a fifth (19.7%) of the blacks were female. Black females were somewhat more likely to be arrested for violence than white females, but the relationship for gender was weak (Cramer's V = .124).

The arrest reports were examined to determine family structure of the arrestees. True to the literature, these youths were likely to come from "broken homes." Family structure was determined by comparing the addresses of father, mother, and youth. On those cases in which all three agreed, it was assumed that the family was not "broken." Obviously, this measure missed cases in which parents were separated in all aspects but official address, so the figures cited below represent minimum levels. A large proportion of the violent youths (41.0%) did not live with both parents or a parent and step-parent. Fewer whites (33.8%) lived with one parent or no-parent homes[6] than blacks (47.1%). Blacks were more likely (37.1%) than whites (22.3%) to live with only their mother. While a large segment of the violent population came from "broken homes," blacks were somewhat more likely to do so than whites.

On about half (49.2%) of the first violent arrests (49.0% for whites, 48.3% for blacks), at least one other youth was involved in the offense. In about a quarter (28.1% overall; 27.5% for whites and 28.5% for blacks) of the arrests, two or more companions were present in the incident. A large percentage of black and white youths engaged in violence in the company of others. Again, these figures represent minimum levels of group participation, since many youths may have had companions who were not apprehended.

The Arrest and Race

The 1956-1958 violent cohort was arrested 3373 times or an average of 4.2 arrests per person. This includes all arrests—violent, property, drug, and status. Whites averaged slightly more arrests than blacks (4.4 compared to 4.0), though the relationship was weak (Cramer's V = .174). Recidivists (two or more arrests) were about equal for whites (71.1%) and blacks (70.1%). White youths were more likely (35.4%) than black youths (31.9%) to be "chronics" (five or more arrests). Wolfgang et al. (1972:

TABLE 1   Distribution of All Violent Arrests by Race (1956-58 cohort)

| Arrest | Race | | | | | |
| | Black | | White | | Total | |
	(N)	%	(N)	%	(N)	%
Murder/Manslaughter	12	80.0	3	20.0	15	100.0
Rape	22	55.0	18	45.0	40	100.0
Unarmed Robbery	161	62.6	96	37.4	257	100.0
Assault	199	53.1	176	46.9	375	100.0
Armed Robbery	72	67.9	34	32.1	106	100.0
Aggravated Assault	44	48.9	46	51.1	90	100.0
Sexual Imposition	49	49.0	51	51.0	100	100.0

Chi Square 23.756 with 8 DF, Sig = .002; Cramer's v. = .156

66-70) reported significantly more arrests for non-whites than whites. The Columbus cohort showed no major differences in the average number of arrests for each racial category. In fact, the findings tend toward the reverse—whites had slightly higher averages and were more likely to be chronics than blacks.

These 811 youths were arrested 985 times for violent offenses or an average of 1.21 arrests per person. Black youths averaged slightly (1.23) more violent arrests than whites (1.16), though the relationship between race and number of violent arrests was weak (Cramer's V = .126). Most (83.5%) youths were arrested only once for violent offenses with blacks (20.6%) somewhat more likely than whites (11.7%) to have multiple violent arrests.

For most youths, violence was a minor part of their entire arrest career. Violent arrests represented only slightly over a quarter (28.8%) of all arrests. Black youths had a slightly higher percentage (30.8%) than whites (26.6%). Only a few youths (31)—4.3% of the blacks and 3.3% of the whites—had three or more violent arrests. Even fewer youths (21) were arrested for two or more "serious" violent offenses (murder/manslaughter, rape, armed robbery, and aggravated assault). Black youths were much more likely than white youths to have multiple serious violent arrests. Fifteen, or 71.4%, of these offenders were black. Since the numbers are very small, these differences must be viewed carefully. The relationship between race and type of violent offense (see Table 1) was statistically weak (Cramer's V = .156). Only for murder/manslaughter and armed robbery were the distributions significantly different from the cohort distribution. Black youths were arrested for four-fifths of the murders and two-thirds of the armed robberies compared to their 55% of the violent population. Since, statistically, the overall relationship was weak, this overrepresentation may be a function of the small numbers involved in these two offenses. Compared to the finding of Wolfgang et al. (1972: 68-69), the differences in the Columbus cohort were minor. (Philadelphia non-whites were arrested for *all* of the murders, 86% of the rapes, 89% of the robberies, 82% of the aggravated assaults, and 67% of the "other assaults").

Offense Dynamics

The "age of onset" refers to the age at which a youth was first arrested (or first arrested for a violent offense in the case of "violent onset"). Small differences were found between the two races. Blacks were first arrested earlier (13.2 years old) than whites (13.4 years old), but the difference was weak (Cramer's V = .134). Blacks were also first arrested for violent offenses earlier than whites (blacks at 14.2 years and whites at 14.5 years, Cramer's V = .113). Thus black juveniles tended to start arrest and violent careers earlier than white juveniles. The differences are slight and could very well be the function of earlier police intervention, so strong conclusions should not be drawn from these findings.

A common belief is that juveniles progress from minor offenses to more serious offenses. To measure whether this happened for the violent cohort, a "position variable" was created.[7] This variable was used to measure whether a violent arrest occurred in the beginning (first third), middle (second third), end (third third), or a combination of these (mixed). Whites and blacks were about equally likely to have a violent arrest in any "third" of their career (see Table 2). Whites were somewhat more likely to be arrested for a violent offense in the first third than blacks. The large differences in the "mixed" categories reflect the lower proportion of white youths with multiple violent arrests. Neither black nor white youths showed a tendency to officially "progress" to violence, but may have begun with it.

"Spacing" refers to the time, in months, between arrests. This variable measures how far apart, in time, arrests were which should provide some

TABLE 2   Distribution of Violent Arrest Positions
by Race (in percentages)

Position	Race	
	Black	*White*
First Third Only	25.0	31.1
Second Third Only	22.1	27.6
Third Third Only	24.2	26.5
Mixed[1]	28.7	14.8
Total	100.0	100.0
(N)	(244)[2]	(196)[2]
Cramer's v. = .131		

1. An arrest occurred in two or more "thirds" or a career
2. All youths with one or two total arrests have been excluded.

indication of a youth's involvement in crime. The closer together the
arrests, the more likely the child has a serious crime problem. Spacing in
this study was computed between several events: (1) the time between
arrests, (2) the time from first arrest to first violent arrest, and (3) the time
between violent arrests. A further modification was to calculate "street-
time" by subtracting any time spent in the Ohio Youth Commission
training schools from the total time between the relevant events. This
determined only the time a youth would have spent "on the streets" and
been more readily available for rearrest.

Table 3 shows the similarity between blacks and whites on the three
spacing measures. Black and white youths were distributed equally for
spacings from first arrest to first violent arrest (Cramer's V = .129). White
youths were slightly more likely to have any arrest and violent arrest closer
together than black youths. The results were not statistically strong,
however (Cramer's V = .149 and .234, respectively). Nearly half (46.5%)
of the white youths, who had multiple arrests for violent offenses, averaged those arrests within 10 months or less of each other (in street time)
compared to a little over a third (35.2%) of the blacks. White youths were
thus slightly more likely to be arrested for violent incidents over a shorter
time span than black youths—an indication of either a more persistent
involvement in violence or an inability to avoid detection.

TABLE 3   Mean Street Spacings[1] Between Arrest Events by Race
(in percentages)

Spacing (in months)	Avg. Street Spacing-All Arrests		Street Spacing First Arrest to First Violent Arrest		Avg. Street Spacing-All Violent Arrests	
	RACE		*RACE*		*RACE*	
	Black	*White*	*Black*	*White*	*Black*	*White*
0-5	25.8	33.3	45.4[2]	44.8[2]	24.2	30.2
6-10	30.0	30.7	7.7	6.9	11.0	16.3
11-15	15.8	15.7	7.1	3.1	20.9	9.3
16-20	8.4	8.4	5.8	6.5	6.6	9.3
21-25	6.1	1.9	6.1	3.8	11.0	7.0
26-50	11.0	7.7	17.7	24.1	17.6	23.3
51-99	2.3	1.9	9.4	10.0	8.8	4.7
100+	0.6	0.4	0.6	0.8	–	–
TOTAL	100.0	100.0	99.8	100.0	100.1	100.1
(N)	(310)	(261)	(310)	(261)	(91)	(43)

All arrests	Cramer's v. = .149
First to First Violent	Cramer's v. = .129
All Violent Arrests	Cramer's v. = .234

[1] This table shows the distribution of mean spacings for each individual's
arrest career for those persons with two or more arrests (or violent arrests).

2 Also includes violent arrests which were also the first arrest (i.e., spacing
of zero months.)

Aftermath of Arrest–Disposition

The disposition for the 1956-1960 cohort was collapsed into four major
categories: institution (commitment to the Ohio Youth Commission),
jail-detention, formal supervision (mainly probation), and informal supervision (e.g., reprimand and release, held open, community agencies).
Blacks were slightly more likely (22.0%) to receive the more severe
sentence of "institution" than whites (18.2%) and less likely (39.9%) to
get "informal supervision" than whites (44.4%; see Table 4). Statistically,
the relationship between race and disposition was very weak (Cramer's
V = .061).

TABLE 4   Distribution of Disposition by Race: Five Birth
Cohorts 1956-60 (1)

| Disposition | Race | | | |
| | Black | | White | |
	(N)	*%*	*(N)*	*%*
Institution (OYC)	406	22.0	295	18.2
Jail-Detention	344	18.7	272	16.8
Formal Supervision	357	19.4	335	20.7
Informal Supervision	735	39.9	720	44.4
Total	1842	100.0	1622	100.1

Cramer's v. = .061

[1] Excludes incomplete and dismissed cases.

Liska and Tausig (1979: 199) discuss the very high numbers of blacks that are sent to training centers. They state that in three separate studies (Ferdinand and Luchterhand, 1970; Thornberry, 1973; Arnold, 1974) percentages of total arrestees who were institutionalized was 85.7, 82.3, and 87.1, respectively. About equal proportions of black arrestees (28.7%) were sent to the training schools as white arrestees (23.7%). A total of 127 blacks and 96 whites were institutionalized for a total of 223 youths from the 1956-1958 cohort. Thus, 56.95% of the youths sent to training schools were black—a figure very close to the black proportion of the violent cohort (54.6%). These figures do not approach the 80% plus figures cited by Liska and Tausig (1974). The differences may be a function of the nature of the populations or different levels of racial bias in different cities. Possibly the use of cross-sectional data in these studies overestimated the level of black institutionalization.

While an individual black was slightly more likely to be institutionalized, individual whites were likely to be sent more often to training schools than blacks. Whites averaged 1.86 trips compared to 1.83 trips for blacks. Again, there were very little differences between races and the relationship was very weak (Cramer's V = .058).

DISCUSSION AND CONCLUSIONS

The literature concerning race and crime has stressed the overinvolvement of blacks in crime. The findings of this study do not challenge that literature. Black involvement in the violent cohort far exceeded their proportion of the Franklin County 1956-1958 birth cohort. Possible reasons for such overrepresentation are many: (1) The Columbus police may have more closely observed black youths or been racially biased in their dealing with black juveniles. (2) Black violent youths had, on the whole, a lower SES than white violent juveniles. Thus selection into the violent population may be more a function of SES than race. (3) More black youths may commit violent offenses than white youths. Any, or all, of the above could be an explanation of this finding.

Simply reporting that blacks are arrested out of proportion to their numbers in the population clouds a much more complex set of findings. Comparison of black and white violent offenders on social and arrest characteristics failed to disclose any statistically substantial correlations. White youths had about the same number of total and violent arrests as blacks. The types of violent arrests were nearly similar for both races. The arrest dynamics (age of onset, position, and spacing) were virtually the same. Dispositions for offenses were also comparable. Social characteristics such as group behavior, family composition, and gender were very similar. It must be acknowledged that the raw frequency distributions did show that blacks were arrested for more violent offenses, first arrested at an earlier age, and more likely to be multiple violent and serious violent repeaters. Conversely, whites averaged more total arrests and were more likely to be "chronics" than blacks. However, the association between race and these variables was weak in every case, except SES in which it approached a moderate level. In short, contrary to other studies such as Wolfgang et al. (1972), this population of black offenders did not significantly differ from white offenders. Though some of the raw findings did support the Wolfgang et al. (1972) findings, the differences did not approach the magnitude of the differences found in the Philadelphia cohort.

The policy implications of this study offset those of the Philadelphia study which concludes (Wolfgang et al., 1972: 112) that if the resources of the justice system were focused on lower SES blacks, the most serious crime would be reduced. The differences between black and white offenders were so slight that little real advantage would be gained from an emphasis on the black (nonwhite) juvenile population. Based on the Columbus findings, there should be no rush to establish a separate anti-delinquency program for blacks.[8]

One further statement should be made regarding black overrepresentation in violent statistics. There is a tendency, especially among the public, to argue that most blacks are violent because they contribute to the crime statistics in numbers four to five times their proportion. This study clearly shows that only a minority of blacks ever come in contact with the police for violence. The black violent cohort represented only 5.6% of the black 1956-1958 birth cohort. Even black males, who make up a majority of violent offenders, constitute only 9.1% of the 1956-1958 black male birth cohort. Over 90% of the black males in this cohort were never arrested for even petty violent offenses. Thus, blacks, per se, are not necessarily violent but only appear so in cross-sectional statistics such as Uniform Crime Report statistics.

Finally, an important conclusion from this study is that very few of these 809 (811 total) youths, black or white, could be truly called "violent delinquents." More accurately most were "delinquents with a violent arrest." Few of these youths were officially repetitively violent and even fewer repeated serious violent offenses. The great bulk of arrests for both races were for nonviolent crime (68% of black arrests and 73% of the white arrests). The majority of violent arrests were for the less serious violent offenses of single assault, sexual imposition, and unarmed robbery (73% of the black violent arrests and 76% of the white violent arrests). While this study is concerned with "violent offenders," it must be recognized that this term may be a misnomer for many of these youths. For many, if not most, of the youths in this study the only unifying criterion is the arbitrary condition of an arrest for violent offenses, not the condition of "being violent."

This study set out to describe the differences and similarities between black and white violent juveniles. It has shown that black violent offenders are very similar to white violent offenders along many lines. More research must be done on this topic to develop an adequate knowledge base about violent juveniles before any policy changes are formulated.

NOTES

1. Liska and Tausig (1979) discuss 17 of these studies which represent many of the major works in this area. They are: Goldman (1963), Terry (1963), Wilson (1968), Wheeler et al. (1968), Gould (1969), Hirshi (1969), Black and Reiss (1970), Ferdinand and Luchterhand (1970), Arnold (1971), Scarpetti and Stephenson (1971), Weiner and Willie (1971), Langby (1972), Williams and Gold (1972) Thornberry (1973), Meade (1974), Thomas and Sieverdes (1975), and Thomas and Cage (1977).

2. For an excellent review of the major works on the violent juvenile, see Doleschal and Newton (1978: 539-573).

3. Base numbers are for Franklin County unless indicated otherwise because youths from anywhere in the county were arrested by the Columbus City Police

within the city limits. Also due to the rapidly changing nature of the city boundary, it was difficult to determine if youths came from Columbus or the surrounding county.

4. One Oriental and one person of nonascertainable race were excluded from the following analysis. This left 809 persons for the study.

5. This method has the obvious disadvantage of assuming that all youths in a tract were at about median income. This technique was the only method available and has been utilized in other studies (Wolfgang et al., 1972).

6. Youths who lived with grandparents, in foster homes, or in Franklin County Children Services group homes were considered to be in "no-parent" homes.

7. Position refers to the occurrence of violent arrest in comparison to all other non-violent arrests. Arrest careers were divided roughly into "thirds." Thirds differed by the number of total arrests. For example, a person with nine total arrests would have had his/her first three arrests comprise their "first third," the second three arrests as the second third and the last three arrests as the third third. If this person's second arrest was for a violent offense and was his/her only violent arrest, then it would have been labeled as the "first third." If his/her seventh arrest had been the only violent arrest, then three "thirds" the career was labeled "mixed." Space limitations preclude a thorough discussion of this and the spacing variable. For a more complete explanation, see Hamparian (1978: 28).

8. Comparison of the Columbus and Philadelphia findings must be viewed carefully. The differences in findings may be attributable to many explanations. The cities may have different police practices or different offender populations. Also, the techniques of the two studies were not totally comparable.

REFERENCES

Arnold, W. R. (1971) "Race and ethnicity relative to other factors in juvenile court dispositions." *American Journal of Sociology,* 77: 211-227.

Black, D. J. and A. J. Reiss, Jr. (1970) "Police control of juveniles." *American Sociological Review,* 35: 63-77.

Chambliss, W. J. and R. H. Nagasawa (1969) "On the validity of official statistics: A comparative study of white, black and Japanese high school boys." *Journal of Research in Crime and Delinquency,* 6: 71-77.

Doleschal, E. and A. Newton (1978) "The violent juvenile." *Criminal Justice Abstracts* 10: 539-573.

Eaton, J. W. and K. Polk (1961) *Measuring Delinquency.* Pittsburgh: University of Pittsburgh Press.

Erickson, M. L. (1973) "Delinquency in a birth cohort: A new direction of criminology research?" *Journal of Criminal Law, Criminology and Police Science* 63: 362-367.

Ferdinand, T. N. and E. G. Luchterhand (1970) "Inner-city youth, the police, the juvenile, court, and justice." *Social Problems* 17: 510-527.

Forslund, M. S. (1966) "Race and crime." Ph.D. Dissertation, Yale University.

Gold, M. and D. J. Teimer (1974) "Changing patterns of delinquent behavior among Americans 13-16 years old: 1967-1972." National Survey of Youth, Report No.

1. University of Michigan, Institute for Social Research. (mimeo)

Goldman, N. (1963) *The Differential Selection of Juvenile Offenders for Court Appearance*. New York: National Council on Crime and Delinquency.

Gould, L. C. (1969) "Who defines delinquency: A comparison of self-reported and officially-reported indices of delinquency for three racial groups." *Social Problems* 16: 325-336.

Hamparian, D., R. L. Schuster, S. Dinitz, and J. P. Conrad (1978) *The Violent Few*. Lexington, MA: Lexington.

Heilbrun, A. B. and K. S. Heilbrun (1977) "The black minority criminal and violent crime: The role of self-control." *British Journal of Criminology*, 17: 370-377.

Hirschi, T. (1969) *Causes of Delinquency*. Berkeley: University of California Press.

Hohenstein, W. F. (1969) "Factors influencing the police disposition of juvenile offenders," Pp. 138-149 in T. Sellin and M. E. Wolfgang (eds.) *Delinquency: Selected Studies*. New York: Wiley.

Illinois Institute for Juvenile Research (1972) *Juvenile Delinquency in Illinois*. Chicago: Illinois Department of Mental Health.

Kelley, C. M. (1975) *Crime in the United States: Uniform Crime Reports*. Washington, DC: Government Printing Office.

Langley, M. H. (1972) "The juvenile court: The making of a delinquent." *Law and Society Review* 7: 273-299.

Levitch, J. A. and L. F. Vlock (1977) "Violent street kids—must it be jail?" *Parade* (May 1): 24.

Liska, A. E. and M. Tausig (1979) "Theoretical interpretations of social class and racial differentials in legal decision-making for juveniles." *Sociological Quarterly*, 20: 197-207.

Meade, A. (1974) "Seriousness of delinquency, the adjudication decision and recidivism: A longitudinal configurational analysis." *Journal of Criminal Law and Criminology* 64: 478-786.

Mulvihill, D. J. and M. M. Trimin (1969) *Crimes of Violence* (Vols. 11-13). Washington, DC: Government Printing Office.

Pope, C. E. (1979) "Race and crime revisited." *Crime and Delinquency* 25: 347-357.

Scarpetti, F. R. and R. M. Stephenson (1971) "Juvenile court dispositions, factor in the decision making process." *Crime and Delinquency* 17: 142-151.

Schuster, R. L. (1978) "Violent juvenile offenders: A longitudinal cohort analysis." Ph.D. dissertation, The Ohio State University.

Short, J. F. and I. F. Nye (1958) "Extent of unrecorded delinquency, tentative conclusions." *Criminal Law, Criminology and Police Science* 49: 296-302.

Strassburg, P. A. (1978) *Violent Delinquents: A Report to the Ford Foundation from the Vera Institute of Justice*. New York: Monarch.

Terry, R. M. (1967) "The screening of juvenile offenders." *Journal of Criminal Law, Criminology and Police Science*, 58: 173-182.

Thomas, C. and R. Cage (1977) "The effects of social characteristics on juvenile court dispositions." *Sociological Quarterly*, 18: 237-252.

Thomas, C. and C. M. Sieverdes (1975) "Juvenile court intake: An analysis of discretionary decision making." *Criminology*, 12: 413-432.

Thornberry, T. P. (1973) "Race, socioeconomic status and sentencing in the juvenile justice system." *Journal of Criminal Law, Criminology and Police Science*, 64: 90-98.

Tracy, P. E. (1978) "An analysis of the incidence and seriousness of self-reported delinquency and crime." Ph.D. dissertation, University of Pennsylvania.

U.S. Bureau of Census (1975) "Estimates of the population of the United States by age, sex and race: 1970 to 1975." *Current Population Reports* (Series P-25, No. 615). Washington, DC: Government Printing Office.

——— (1970) "Census of population and housing: 1970 census tracts (Final Report PHC (1)–50 Columbus, Ohio SMSA). Washington, DC: Government Printing Office.

Vera Institute of Justice (1976) "Violent delinquents." (unpublished)

Weiner, N. L. and C. V. Willie (1971) "Decisions by juvenile officers." *American Journal of Sociology,* 77: 1-12.

Wheeler, S., E. Bonacich, M. R. Cramer, and I. K. Zola (1968) "Delinquency prevention and organizational relations." Pp. 31-60 in S. Wheeler (ed.) *Controlling Delinquents.* New York: Wiley.

Williams, J. R. and M. Gold (1972) "From delinquent behavior to official delinquency." *Social Problems,* 20: 209-229.

Wilson, J. Q. (1968) "The police and the delinquent to official delinquency " Pp. 9-30 in S. Wheeler (ed.) *Controlling Delinquents.* New York: Wiley.

Wolfgang, M. E. (1958) *Patterns in Criminal Homicide.* Philadelphia: University of Pennsylvania Press.

——— R. M. Figlio and T. Sellin *Delinquency in a Birth Cohort.* Chicago: University of Chicago Press.

7

JUVENILE COURT DISPOSITIONS OF STATUS OFFENDERS:
An Analysis of Case Decisions

William Feyerherm

Criminal Justice Program
School of Social Welfare
University of Wisconsin—Milwaukee

Official statistics regarding crime and delinquency suggest that Blacks and other disadvantaged segments of the population are differentially involved in criminal events. Overrepresentation in arrest, conviction, and prison statistics of such groups has been documented repeatedly in a wide variety of studies (Pope, 1979). Recent victimization survey results have also shown non-whites to be overrepresented with respect to their population base in common law personal crimes of robbery, rape, and assault (Hindelang, 1978). Although there are a variety of methodological shortcomings and other distortions that may question the validity of these fidings, most attentions has focused upon the problem of selection bias in the identification and recording of criminal incidents (McNeely and Pope, 1978). It is frequently argued, for example, that decisions occuring within the criminal justice system are based on extralegal criteria in that the system treats certain categories of offenders less favorably than others. In speaking to the issue of Black overinvolvement, Korn and McCorkle note:

> A large but unknown portion of this higher rate of involvement with law enforcement must be attributed to distortions introduced into the statistics by differential legal and penal treatment of Negroes. There is no way of determining whether the higher Negro rate represents a higher rate of actual crime or a greater liability to involvement with law-enforcement agencies. [1961: 245].

Theoretical support for this argument has been found in the labelling perspective which argues that differential processing of offenders based upon ascribed characteristics is to be expected. Becker (1963) and Schur (1971) argue that it is precisely because of ascribed characteristics that certain population segments are stereotyped and defined as criminal. Kobrin (1972) notes:

> The rise to prominence of labeling theory in recent years represents a major development in the analysis of deviant behavior. The particular contribution of the theory has been to call attention to the fact that deviant behavior is always and necessarily a joint product of acts and definition of acts, of the conduct of actors and the definition of that conduct by others as contravening some set of social norms.

The issues raised by the differential involvement thesis and the labelling perspective are probably seldom more prominent than in the handling of "status" offenders in juvenile justice system. Typically those statutes defining status offenses are less specific in defining the behavioral elements required for adjudication. As a result this category of juvenile offense appears to provide the greatest potential for the exercise of discretion by juvenile justice decision makers, and consequently the greatest potential for the type of differential decision making described by many theorists. Status offenses generally include those acts committed by juveniles which would not be subject to criminal law had they been adults. These acts include truancy, running away from home, incorrigibility, and the like. These offenders are doubly stigmatized in being defined as "delinquent" for acts which would not come under the purview of criminal law had they not been under a legally prescribed age. Often quasi-delinquent labels such as CHINS (child-in-need-of-supervision) and PINS (person-in-need-of-supervision) are used to describe this special category of juvenile delinquent. Twenty-five states currently use such quasi-delinquent labels while the remaining states classify them as delinquent and award them similar dispositions as children having committed criminal acts (Katkin et al., 1976).

In spite of the apparently less serious nature of status offense, it would be mistaken to assume that this category of offenses is treated more lightly than others by the juvenile justice system. It has been estimated that over one quarter of all delinquents in correctional institutions are there for status offenses (Sheridan, 1967). More conservative estimates place the percentage of juveniles incarcerated "in need of supervision" as approximately 10% of juveniles incarcerated, although this percentage is as high as 30% for some states (Parisi et al., 1979: 612). Further, approximately one-fifth of the males but over half of the females in juvenile detention homes are held for status offenses. Some research has shown that status offenders are more likely to be institutionalized than those juveniles who have committed a legally defined criminal act (Lerman, 1973). Similarly, with regard to length of incarceration, status offenders receive more severe treatment compared to their counterparts committing "adult" offenses (Lerman, 1973). This is especially curious since public opinion research indicates that the general public considers status offenses to be less serious than all other types of offenses (Rossi et al., 1974). In light of these factors, this article focuses on the processing of juvenile status offenders through selected decision points in the California juvenile justice system. Primary attention is given to the degree to which race and other extralegal factors influence decisions regarding status offenders.

PREVIOUS RESEARCH

With regard to the processing of juvenile offenders, Platt (1969), Martin (1970), and Schur (1973) maintain that dispositions are frequently based on social attributes rather than legal criteria. As Schur notes:

> In our society, lower class children more than middle class ones, Black children more than White ones, and boys more than girls, face high probabilities (i.e., run a special categorical risk in the actuarial sense) not only of engaging in rule violation in the first place, but also of becoming enmeshed in official negative labeling processes [1973: 125-126].

Results from empirical research focusing upon juvenile justice dispositions have been far less conclusive. Terry (1967), in examining juvenile court dispositions in Racine, Wisconsin, found no evidence of racial or social class bias with regard to severity of disposition. However, in a similar study, Arnold (1971) found that even when controlling for such factors as the marital status of the juvenile's parents, seriousness of the offense, number and seriousness of prior and concurrent offenses, and delinquency rate of the offender's neighborhood, there were substantial racial and ethnic differences in recorded dispositions. Consistent with this study, Thornberry (1973) found significant racial and social class differences with regard to the disposition of juvenile offenders in Philadelphia.

In perhaps the most comprehensive analysis of juvenile court dispositions to date, Cohen (1975a, 1975b) was unable to find evidence of race or social class bias once appropriate control variables were introduced. Utilizing data obtained from Denver County (Colorado), Memphis-Shelby County (Tennessee), and Montgomery County (Pennsylvania) juvenile courts, Cohen examined preadjudicatory detention and delinquency dispositions isolating those factors leading to the more severe outcomes. Regression and predictive attribute analysis showed that previous court referrals, present activity (e.g., idleness), and family stability were the most important factors influencing detention decisions. Similarly, severity of case dispositions were primarily accounted for by prior processing decisions. In concluding, Cohen (1975a: 43) states: "Our analysis gives no indication that minorities or lower status youths are discriminated against in any of the courts once controls are introduced into the analysis."

While this study did not reveal extralegal factors to be of primary importance in the processing of juveniles, there were, however, substantial differences between status and other offense types (Cohen, 1975). In Denver County, for example, approximately 25% of all youths placed in detention were charged with the commission of status offenses (CHINS). More startling differences were shown in detention decisions occurring in Montgomery County. Here over 50% of thos detained were charged with status offenses (unruly). This represented the highest detention rate of any offense type, more than double the rate for those charged with violent offenses.

An examination of these and other studies suggests several factors which need further exploration in the study of racial differentiation in juvenile justice processing.[1] First, most studies have examined a single decision point in the juvenile justice system. The expectation appears to be that blatant evidences of racial differentiation will be discovered. In some instances, for example, the Arnold and Thornberry studies, significant differences are found, in others these blatant effects are not found in the examination of a single decision point. This type of analysis, however, overlooks the fact that juveniles are processed by a system composed of multiple decision points. From the perspective of the juvenile, it is the combined effect of these decisions which is of concern. An analysis of possible racial differentiations should likewise be concerned with multiple decision points.

This concern should address two possible circumstances. The first is that the blatant differences sought in earlier studies may be found in different decision locations in the system for different types of cases. For example, in cases of incorrigibility, the decisions made at intake may exhibit differentiation, while such effects might not occur until disposition for other types of cases. For the researcher examining either decision point singly, inconsistent patterns would emerge, confusing and confounding the search for racial differentiations. The second possibility is that no single decision point may exhibit these blatant evidences of differentiation, but that the additive effect of small differences at each decision point may serve to create an overall condition of differential processing. In such a circumstance, the examination of single decision points would lead to a conclusion that only minimal (and probably insignificant) differentiation exists.

A second major factor to be considered in further exploration is the effect of combining jurisdictions. As Cohen's studies indicate, the processing of juveniles may be expected to vary widely across differing jurisdictions. Such variations may serve to confound the search for racial differentiation on two separate fashions. First, following the logic expressed above, racial differentiation may find expression in different locations in the juvenile justice systems of specific jurisdictions. The statistical evidences of such differentiation would thus become diluted when the jurisdictions are treated as an aggregate, particularly if a single decision point was the focus of analysis.

A second confounding effect of combining jurisdictions has to do with the structure of most statistical tests. In nearly all tests, whether correlations or tests of statistical significance, the starting point in the analysis is a measure of the variation of the phenomenon under study (i.e., the dependent variable or the decision outcome as in the present study). The effect of combining several jurisdictions is to increase the variability in decision making, since jurisdictions often use substantially different levels of certain outcomes (as in Cohen's work showing the differences in use of detention between three jurisdictions). In a statistical sense, this means that the original estimate of the variation in the dependent variable would be substantially larger than if each jurisdiction is treated separately. Since the explanatory power of race is not likely to increase with such an aggregation process (and may be expected to decrease following arguments made above), the net effect is to decrease the apparent effect of race on decision making.

CALIFORNIA JUVENILE JUSTICE DATA

In order to further investigate allegations of differential treatment of juvenile status offenders, data were obtained from the state of California for the year 1972. These data include each new delinquent case referred to the probation department and those cases in which a delinquent petition is filed on a currently active dependent case. Thus, these data reflect initial probation intake determinations. All juveniles referred to 10 county probation departments during a one-year period serve as the base for this analysis.[2]

The category covering juvenile status offenses within California is quite broad and ill-defined. Section 601 of the California Welfare and Institutions Code provides that:

> Any person under the age of 18 years who persistently or habitually refuses to obey the reasonable and proper orders or directions of his parents, guardian, custodian or school authorities, or who is beyond the control of such person, or any person who is a habitual truant from school within the meaning of any law of this State, or who from any cause is in danger of leading an idle, dissolute, lewd or immoral life, is within the jurisdiction of the juvenile court which may adjudge such persons to be a ward of the court [Amended Ch. 1748, Stats. 1971. Effective Mar. 4, 1972].

COHORT CHARACTERISTICS

The data as provided by California subdivide status offenders into several categories, four of which had sufficient numbers for statistical analysis. These categories are: incorrigible, truant, runaway, and curfew violations. As a first step in the analysis of processing of status offenders,

TABLE 1   Comparison of Status and Non-Status Offenders on Other Case Variables, in Percent

	Incorrigible	Truant	Runaway	Curfew	Non-status
Referral source:					
Law enforcement	75.3	22.5	95.8	99.7	99.3
School	9.8	74.2	.3	.1	.4
Parents	21.2	3.4	3.9	.2	.3
N	9,731	3,579	9,653	1,871	54,374
Detention:					
Yes	78.5	16.2	84.1	52.6	45.2
No	21.5	83.8	15.9	47.4	54.8
N	7,225	2,395	8,071	1,579	42,823
Intake Disposition:					
Closed	29.8	32.9	64.0	82.7	40.2
Informal	13.7	24.0	8.4	6.8	14.9
Formal	56.4	43.2	27.6	10.5	44.9
N	11,079	3,748	10,497	1,919	58,183
Court Disposition:					
Closed	12.2	6.5	21.4	21.2	16.9
Probation w/o wardship	5.2	8.7	6.1	14.6	12.4
Formal supervision (incl CYA)	82.5	84.8	72.4	64.2	70.7
N	6,499	1,729	3,039	212	26,060

the distributions of status offenders were compared with other categories of juveniles referred to the probation departments. Table 1 provides a summary of these comparisons.[3] In Table 1, all other categories of offense are combined under the heading "nonstatus." There appear to be substantive differences in the manner in which status offenders are handled as compared with nonstatus offenders. With the exception of curfew violations, there is a much higher likelihood that a status offender would come from a referral source other than law enforcement. Parents and schools account for nearly two-fifths of the referrals for incorrigibility for instance, as compared to less than one-tenth of the nonstatus referrals.

Of equal, if not greater, importance are decisions regarding detention prior to intake determinations.[4] Here there are marked differences within the status offenses. Truants were seldom detained (16.2%), while juveniles referred for incorrigibility and runaway were detained (incarcerated) at rates of 78.5% and 84.1% respectively. These rates were substantially above the 47% rate of detention for nonstatus offenders and substantially higher than many of the more serious of the nonstatus offenses such as assault (55.1%), auto theft (64.7%), and drug-related offenses (55.2%).

With regard to the disposition of the case, the probation offices had available three general options: closing the case, handling the case informally, or filing a formal petition of delinquency. There is again a substantial variation within the set of status offenders, with closing the case being most usual for runaways and curfew violations. Truancy is the category (of all offenses) to make greatest use of the informal petitions than the nonstatus cases. In fact, only assault cases had a higher rate (58%) and this is not substantially different.

Once the case has passed from the probation office to the juvenile court three general dispositions were used by the courts in California. These were: closing the case, placing the juvenile on probation without establishing wardship of the state, and establishing formal supervision of the juvenile (including referrals to the California Youth Authority). Table 1 presents the use of these options. Compared to nonstatus offenders, two categories of status offenders were substantially more likely to receive a finding of formal supervision (incorrigible and truancy) while a third (runaway) had a slightly higher likelihood of formal supervision. Only those few cases (212) which reached the juvenile court for curfew violations were less likely to receive formal supervision (64.2%).

PROCESSING OF STATUS OFFENDERS

In examining the processing of status offenders, the issue raised earlier concerns the extent to which the various characteristics of the juvenile influence the processing decisions. The analysis here concentrates on juveniles referred for a status offense and examines two decision points: the initial intake decision and the court disposition. Table 2 displays the impact which various aspects of the juvenile and the case have upon the initial intake decision. By way of summary, it can be said that females, older juveniles, and non-whites (particulary Blacks) are more likely to have petitions filed and correspondingly less likely to have their cases closed.

Just as there were variations in the use of status offenses, there were substantial variations accross jurisdictions in the decisions regarding status offenders. The differences are displayed in Table 2. The rate of formal petitions ranges from 22% to 59%, the use of informal probation ranges from 4% to 27%. While some of this variation may be accounted for through variation in offense mix in counties, it still represents an enormous range of variation in dispositions used by the counties.

TABLE 2   Initial Intake Determination by Case Variables for
Status Offenses only, in Percent

	Closed	*Informal*	*Formal*	*N*
		Determination		
Race:				
White	48.3	11.6	40.1	22,027
Mexican-American	39.0	15.4	45.6	3,386
Black	40.4	9.1	50.5	1,826
Sex:				
Male	49.9	12.2	37.9	14,168
Female	43.5	12.3	44.2	14,585
Age:				
17 and older	42.5	11.5	45.9	10,149
under 17	48.8	12.6	38.5	18,585
Jurisdiction:				
A	58.1	12.7	29.2	456
B	36.1	4.1	59.8	5,585
C	51.8	25.8	22.4	3,345
D	36.5	7.2	56.3	3,434
E	55.7	7.6	36.7	6,076
F	40.3	27.0	32.8	1,395
G	51.3	24.5	24.2	1,822
H	43.5	6.3	50.2	2,271
I	46.7	19.8	33.5	3,276
J	68.4	4.8	26.8	1,092

The second decision point examined in this study is the disposition of the cases by the juvenile court. Of course those cases which were closed at intake are excluded from this analysis, which means that this set of cases already shows the selection effects of the intake process. Nonetheless, the results displayed in Table 3 continue to show some differential probabilities of various dispositions. Age differentials appear to have disappeared, but sex and race differentials are consistent with those displayed in Table 2, although the magnitude of the differences is smaller. Females are more likely to receive a disposition of formal supervision, as are non-whites (especially Blacks). Those cases referred by law enforcement agencies show lower likelihood of formal supervision (76.2%) compared to those referred by either school authorities (84.2%) or parents (88.5%), although some of these differences may be accounted for by differences in types of offense.

TABLE 3   Court Dispositions by Case Variables for Status Offenses only, in Percent

| | Disposition | | |
	Closed	Probation w/o wardship	Formal Supervision
Race:			
White	15.3	6.3	78.3	9153
Mexican-American	11.4	6.9	81.7	1674
Black	11.4	4.5	84.2	942
Sex:			
Male	16.6	6.7	76.6	5582
Female	12.3	5.8	81.8	6730
Age:			
17 and older	13.6	6.2	80.1	4977
under 17	14.6	6.3	79.0	7335
Jurisdiction:			
A	30.7	3.3	66.0	150
B	13.5	5.5	81.0	3261
C	18.5	12.7	68.8	914
D	9.3	2.3	88.5	1923
E	18.3	4.2	77.5	2156
F	21.8	3.8	74.4	532
G	21.0	12.9	65.9	599
H	14.0	4.0	81.9	1139
I	8.2	10.6	81.2	1323
J	4.4	15.9	79.7	315

The greatest variation in the use of dispositional options occurs across jurisdictions. Several of the counties showed a rate of formal supervison of approximately 66%, while others had rates approaching 90%. While portions of the variation may be explained by such variables as type of offense, it is interesting to note that those counties which have the highest rate of filing of formal petitions (Table 2) also tend to have the highest rate of formal supervision as a disposition (Table 3). Thus, the two decision points serve to amplify the effects of one another.

Given that substantial jurisdictional differences have been found in the data set and that there are substantial differences inn outcomes by type of offense (Table 1), it is necessary to further examine the analysis of racial effects presented in Tables 2 and 3 by introducing controls for jurisdiction and offense. In doing so, Tables 4 and 5 have been constructed. These

TABLE 4   Rate of Filing Petitions at Intake for Non-White
Juveniles, Expressed as Deviations from Rate for
Whites, by Offense and County

County	Race	Offense Incorrigible	Truant	Runaway	Curfew
A	M	- .04	.13	.08	.04
	B	– [a]	- -	.01	–
B	M	- .03	.08	.05	.06
	B	.03	.15	- .05	.17
C	M	.00	.06	.16	- .01
	B	- .10	.29	- .01	.00
D	M	.11	- .03	.03	.20
	B	.04	- .06	.01	–
E	M	.11	- .23	.02	- .01
	B	.07	.11	.14	- .02
F	M	.03	.08	.12	–
	B	- .07	.09	.11	–
G	M	.09	.14	.15	- .01
	B	.02	–	.02	–
H	M	.00	.05	.13	- .03
	B	.04	- .02	.29	.05
I	M	.21	.00	.26	.00
	B	.03	.00	.12	–
J	M	–	.14	–	- .05
	B	- .23	–	- .17	- .05
Total	M	.04	- .05	.07	- .01
	B	.04	.16	.07	- .01

[a] Combinations having too few cases for analysis are represented by –.

show the rates of the use of the most formal option available at each
decision point (i.e., the filing of a formal petition at intake and a disposition of formal supervision). In order to facilitate the examination of racial
differences, these rates have been expressed as deviations from the rate for
white juveniles. Thus a rate of .10 for Blacks in Table 4 would mean that
for that particular offense and county, Black juveniles have a rate of
petitions filed which is 10 percentage points higher than the comparable
rate for white juveniles. Likewise an entry of - .10 reflects a lower rate of
petitions filed.

TABLE 5   Rate of Disposition of Formal Supervision, for
Non-white Youth, Expressed as Deviations from
Rate of White Youth, by County and Offense[a]

County	Race	Incorrigible	Offense Truant	Runaway
A	M	-.15	—	—
	B	—	—	—
B	M	.01	.04	.01
	B	.04	—	—
C	M	.04	-.10	.02
	B	.09	-.15	.05
D	M	.05	.04	.01
	B	-.06	.09	—
E	M	-.05	-.12	-.06
	B	.04	.03	.14
F	M	.19	.07	.18
	B	.12	—	—
G	M	.01	.16	.18
	B	—	—	.10
H	M	.04	.01	.38
	B	.06	.00	.29
I	M	-.01	.10	.10
	B	.04	—	.04
J	M	—	—	—
	B	—	—	—
Total	M	.01	.03	.05
	B	.04	.04	.06

[a] In each County, there were too few cases of curfew violation to warrant analysis.

[b] Combinations having too few cases for analysis are represented by —.

Recalling an earlier discussion, three forms of racial differentiation may be expected to appear in a joint examination of Tables 4 and 5. The first may be termed partial differentiation, in which jurisdiction may show differentiation in some offense types but not in others. A relatively clear example of this pattern occurs in the treatment of Blacks in County B (Table 4). For two offense categories the difference between the Black and white rates of petitions filed is minimal (incorrigible = .03, runaway = -.05). For the other two categories, the difference is rather large (truant =

.15, curfew = .17). Since the corresponding figures for Table 5 are either low or negative, there is little evidence of amplification. Thus in some types of offenses, County B appears to have differential processing, while for others no such differential appears.

The second type of differential we may expect might be termed mixed. Like the partial differentiation, a county does not appear to differentiate uniformly at any one decision point, but additionally there appears to be a balancing across decision points, so that if differentiation does not occur at one decision point, it is picked up at the next. Consider, for example, the rate in both Tables 4 and 5 for Mexican-American youth in County I. For those youth referred as incorrigible, the differential rate occurs at intake (.21) while the disposition rate shows no differential treatment (-.01). For truants, the pattern reverses, with no differential treatment at intake (.00) and differential handling at disposition (.10).

The last pattern which might occur is amplification, where some level of differential treatment occurs at each decision point, which logically means that the net effect is greater differential treatment when both decision points are considered simultaneously. As an example, consider the experiences of Black youth in County E. In each of the four categories in Table 4 they are more likely to have a petition filed. Moreover, in each of the categories of Table 5 they are more likely to receive a disposition of formal supervision. Clearly, the amplification is greatest for those youth referred as runaways, but amplification occurs to some degree in each category.

This discussion does not presume that in all counties for all offenses differential treatment takes place. The intent of the foregoing has been to illustrate that racial differentiation may take several forms and that the search for evidences of differential handling may need to look within specific jurisdictions and specific offense categories. Moreover, the combined effect of several decisions must be examined closely, However, it is clear that the rates of differential handling given for the total set of cases work to mask considerable variations in patterns of handling juvenile offenders among the various counties.

DECISION PROCESSES—A MULTIVARIATE VIEW

In an effort to disentangle many of the multivariate relationships, an analysis of covariance approach was utilized. In this approach the depen-

TABLE 6   Multiple Classification Analysis of Intake Determination
by other Case Variables, with Age and Sex as Covariates

	Unadjusted Deviation	ETA	Adjusted Deviation	Beta
Race:				
White	-.01		-.01	
Mexican-American	.04		.06	
Black	.09		.06	
		.06		.06
Referral source:				
Law enforcement	-.03		-.01	
School	.09		.04	
Parents	.15		.01	
		.13		.03
Offense:				
Incorrigible	.15		.17	
Truant	.05		.01	
Runaway	-.13		-.12	
Curfew	-.29		.06	
		.31		.30
Jurisdiction:				
A	-.12		-.09	
B	.19		.22	
C	-.17		-.15	
D	.15		.10	
E	-.06		-.05	
F	-.08		-.12	
G	-.18		-.18	
H	.07		.04	
I	-.11		-.13	
J	-.14		-.07	
		.28		.28
Multiple R				.429

dent variables (intake determination and court disposition) were dichoto-
mized into formal treatments versus closed and informal. Age and sex,
both dichotomies, were treated as covariate while race, offense, referral
source, and jurisdiction were treated as main factors.[5] Each of the
variables was related to disposition. The multiple classification analyses
presented in Tables 6 and 7 summarize these multivariate relationships.
Overall, this collection of variables produces a multiple correlation of .429

TABLE 7   Multiple Classification Analysis of Court Disposition
of Status Offenses by Other Case Variables, with
Sex and Age Covariates

	Unadjusted Deviations	Eta	Adjusted Deviations	Beta
Race:				
White	-.01		-.01	
Mexican-American	.02		.03	
Black	.05		.05	
		.05		.05
Referral Source:				
Law Enforcement	-.03		-.02	
Schools	.06		.01	
Parents	.10		.07	
		.12		.07
Offense:				
Incorrigible	.03		.03	
Truant	.06		.04	
Runaway	-.08		-.07	
Curfew	-.15		-.13	
		.13		.12
Jurisdiction:				
A	-.16		-.15	
B	.05		.04	
C	-.10		-.09	
D	.10		.08	
E	-.03		-.04	
F	-.06		-.06	
G	-.15		-.14	
H	.02		-.02	
I	-.01		.00	
J	.03		.04	
		.16		.15
Multiple R				.233

with the intake determination and .233 with the court disposition. While
the beta coefficients indicate that offense is the largest contributor, it is
also clear that after controlling for all other factors, there are major
differences between counties. While age, sex, and race differences are
found to be important, they are substantially less important than the
jurisdiction.

With regard to racial categorizations, the introduction of control variables, including offense and jurisdiction, diminishes only slightly the differentials between races. The range of deviations from the grand mean dropped from .10 to .07 with regard to the proportion of cases in which the intake determination was to file a formal petition of delinquency and did not change for the court dispositions. Thus, the racial differentials are stable, even when controls are introduced.

CONCLUSION

This study began with an examination of a theoretical framework which argues that extralegal criteria may be critical in the processing of delinquents, particulary criteria such as race. Moreover, the category of status offenders represents the point of clearest ideological clash between those who would view the juvenile justice system in a favorable, paternalistic light and those such as conflict and labelling theorists. From the analysis presented herein, it is clearly the case that the application of the label *status offender* is tied to extralegal characteristics. Moreover, analyses of the processing decisions in these cases confirm the existence of substantive differences in processing, sex, and race groupings. Moreover, it is important to note that the differences in processing are parallel for the two processing decisions examined in this study. That is, the apparent biases in the decision processes serve to amplify the effects of each other, rather than to offset each other. For example, the likelihood of a Black youth apprehended for a status offense receiving formal supervision as a court disposition is 42.5% (likelihood of a formal petition filed [50.5%] multiplied by the likelihood of formal supervision [84.2%], while the likelihood of a white youth receiving formal supervision is 31.4%. This creates a difference of 11.1% in the overall handing of the two types of cases, which is greater than the percentage difference occurring in either of the decision points examined singly. Moreover, this amplification process, if it occurs at additional points in the processing of cases, would result in a situation in which the overall operation of the juvenile justice system would have the effect of introducing substantial biases in the treatment of classes of juveniles (especially minorities). However, an examination of biases at any single stage of the process would not reveal major evidence of biases. In short, while there is not evidence of blatant discrimination in these data, there is a suggestion of accumulations of discrimination, which collectively may have the same results.

In some important ways the findings here parallel the findings of Strasburg (1978). Dealing with violent delinquents, Strasburg found distinct patterns and differences in the handling of delinquents across counties. Indeed, his analysis shows that decisions regarding violent delinquents are strongly associated with the size of the jurisdiction and the structure of the court system in which the case is disposed. His analysis also indicated the possibility of racial differences in the processing of violent delinquents. In a similar fashion, although factors such as age, sex, and race are herein shown to be related to processing decisions, by far the greatest contributor (aside from offense category) was the jurisdiction. In essence, then, *where* one is may be as important as *who* that person is or *what* that person has done. Particularly in such an ill-defined area as status offenses, such findings should cause considerable concern about the equity of the system.

NOTES

1. For an additional review of these factors, see the introductory chapter for this volume.

2. The 10 counties were selected by the Bureau of Criminal Statistics for pilot implementation of an OBTS style information system. This system is the source of the data used in this study.

3. Since the cases studied represent the population of cases in these counties rather than a sample, traditional tests of statistical significance are not appropriate nor are they reported.

4. As indicated in Table 1 and following tables, there were a significant number of cases for which the detention decision was either unknown or not recorded in the data system. These cases have been treated as missing in the analysis of detention decisions.

5. Detention was excluded from the multivariate analysis because its use would have depleted the number of cases available for analysis.

REFERENCES

Arnold, W. R. (1971) "Race and ethnicity relative to other factors in juvenile court dispositions." *American Journal of Sociology*, 77: 211-222.

Becker, H. (1963) *The Outsiders.* New York: Free Press.

Cohen, L. E. (1975a) "Pre-adjudicatory detention in three juvenile courts: An empirical analysis of the factors related to detention decision outcomes." Analytic Report SD-AR-8. Washington, DC: Department of Justice, Law Enforcement Assistance Administration, National Criminal Justice Information and Statistics Service.

――― (1975b) "Delinquency dispositions: An empirical analysis of processing decisions in three juvenile courts." Analytic Report SD-AR-9. Washington, DC: Department of Justice, Law Enforcement Assistance Administration, National Criminal Justice Information and Statistics Service.

Hindelang, M. J. (1978) "Race and involvement in common law personal crimes: A comparison of three techniques." *American Sociological Review*, 42: 93-109.

Katkin, D., D. Hyman, and J. Kramer (1976) *Juvenile delinquency and the Juvenile Justice System.* North Scituate, MA: Duxbury.

Kobrin, S. (1972) "The labeling approach: Problems and limits." In J. F. Short, Jr. (ed.) *Delinquency, Crime and Society.* Chicago: University of Chicago Press.

Korn, R. R. and L. W. McCorkle (1961) *Criminology and Penology.* New York: Holt, Rinehart and Winston.

Lerman, P. (1973) "Delinquents without crimes." In A. S. Blumberg (ed.) *The Scales of Justice.* New Brunswick, NJ: Transaction.

Martin, J. J. (1970) *Toward a Political Definition of Delinquency.* Washington, DC: Government Printing Office.

McNeely, R. L. and C. E. Pope (1978) "Race and involvement in common law personal crime: A response to Hindelang." *Review of Black Political Economy.*

Parisi, N., M. Gottfredson, M. J. Hindelang, and T. Flanagan (1979) *Sourcebook of Criminal Justice Statistics–1978.* Washington, DC: Government Printing Office.

Platt, A. (1969) *The Child Savers: The Invention of Delinquency.* Chicago: University of Chicago Press.

Pope, C. E. (1979) "Race and crime revisited." *Crime and Delinquency*, 25: 347-357.

Rossi, P. H. (1974) "The seriousness of crimes: Normative structure and individual differences." *American Sociological Review*, 39: 224-237.

Schur, E. (1973) *Radical Non-intervention: Rethinking the Delinquency Problem.* Englewood Cliffs, NJ: Prentice-Hall.

――― (1971) *Labeling Deviant Behaviors.* New York: Harper & Row.

Sheridan, W. H. (1967) "Juveniles who commit noncriminal acts: Why treat in a correctional system?" *Federal Probation*, 31: 26-30.

Strasburg, P. A. (1978) *Violent Delinquents: A Report to the Ford Foundation from the Vera Institute of Justice.* New York: Monarch.

Terry, R. M. (1967) "The screening of juvenile offenders." *Journal of Criminal Law, Criminology and Police Science*, 58: 173-181.

Thornberry, T. P. (1973) "Race, socioeconomic status and sentencing in the juvenile justice system." *Journal of Criminal Law & Criminology*, 64: 90-98.

IV.

Proposals for Change:
Two Examples

Innovative attempts to achieve a more viable system of criminal justice must take into account the fact that basic cultural differences exist between racial minority groups and the dominant majority-group population. Ameliorative attempts must also be based on the recognition that fundamental cultural differences exist among various minority groups. Pointing out that strong mechanisms for social control based upon kinship and other patterns are likely to exist in minority communities, Parnell urges their involvement with the legal system to enhance the management of criminal offenses. He emphasizes that to ignore the existence of these networks creates conflicts when outsiders, including legal authorities, attempt to impose their views.

In making these points the author relies heavily on an ethnographic study of the "Flats," a Black neighborhood located in a midwestern city. He briefly describes various patterns by which internal neighborhood control over certain aspects of community life are orchestrated and maintained. In his account of Flats community life, the author identifies several potential strengths and weaknesses associated with the incorporation of local control mechanisms into the formal legal system and concludes that the strengths of both systems may be "fitted" together to achieve optimal social control and legal justice.

Using a second case study, Parnell describes how one system involving local participation in judicial decision making operates in Oaxaca, Mexico.

Parnell details the conflicts and problems that exist between the local legal structure, staffed by indigenous citizens who adjudicate/mediate disputes on the basis of community norms and state officials who adjudicate on the basis of formally and officially specified legal codes. Despite the numerous problems the author identifies, he suggests that such problems merely argue for legal decentralization that is more carefully planned. He concludes his discussion by offering several guidelines which help to avoid some of the problems that may accompany "community-controlled" alternatives.

Debro presents a number of critical issues concerning the education of Black students in criminology and criminal justice from a historical and contemporary framework. The author notes, for example, that although the proliferation of criminal justice and criminology educational programs can be attributed to the Black population (e.g., ghetto riots), Blacks have not been the beneficiaries of these programs. Essentially, the Law Enforcement Assistance Administration was created to deal with "Black Lawlessness" of the 1960s, yet the beneficiaries of educational incentives were whites who in turn supported a white-dominated crime-control establishment. Traditional Black colleges and universities have not received adequate funding to advance criminology/criminal justice education, especially at the graduate level. For example, Debro notes that prior to 1978 there were no criminology or criminal justice educational programs at the graduate level in Black colleges. Similarly, within criminology and criminal justice, there are very few role models for prospective students within the Black community. Debro concludes by outlining present and future steps that need to be undertaken in order to create a critical mass of Black professionals who are concerned with criminal justice issues and who, as professionals, will contribute scholarly and racially sensitive perspectives to the field.

8

COMMUNITY JUSTICE
VERSUS CRIME CONTROL

Philip Parnell

Indiana University

The realization that individuals from different cultures will respond differently to the same laws and legal mechanisms is as old as the thoughts of
Montesquieu (1750) and as recent as Silberman's (1978) attack on the
"culture of poverty" approach (Lewis, 1959) to explaining the relatively
high frequency of Black crimes of violence in the United States.

Montesquieu noted two dynamics of law which are integral to understanding Black social control in the context of American criminal justice
systems. They are that the relations between (state) law and the customs
of citizens are "the crucial criterion of legal justice" (Pospisil, 1971: 131)
and that "formal" law and other systems of social control "although
analytically and formally distinguishable, are mutually dependent,"
(Pospisil, 1971: 136).

In a similar vein, Silberman attributes the disproportionately frequent
involvement of Blacks in violent American crime to the violent history of
contact between black culture and the predominant white culture in the
United States and to the breakdown of internal social control which
previously resulted from the cohesiveness of Black communities and the
force of oral culture.

In an implicit criticism of Wolfgang's (1967) "subculture of violence"
approach, Silberman argues that some Blacks are violent not merely
because they are members of a racial minority group and oppressed by the
majority population but also because Black oppression has been accom-

plished through means more violent than those experienced by other national minority groups. He claims that the process of integration begun in the 1950s has weakened the Black cultural and social mechanisms which both channeled and inhibited Black rage.

Silberman's argument is ambiguous, however, for he claims integration has resulted in more homogeneously poor black communities. He implies that the poorer Black communities, as a result of migration of upwardly mobile Blacks, are more socially disorganized than those which were economically heterogeneous.

Closer examination of a subsistence level Black community in the United States by the anthropologist Carol Stack (1974) illustrates that the community has established and maintains an extensive system of internal control across networks of kin and friends. If other subsistence level Black communities have developed such internal control systems, it may then be the mutual independence of community styles of authority attribution and the style of assumption and assertion of authority within the criminal justice system which, as Montesquieu suggests, contributes to the over-representation of Blacks in crime statistics.

Before proceeding with a discussion of Stack's findings, I would like to state an assumption which I believe is basic to understanding the operation of criminal justice systems in multicultural societies such as the United States:

> When two distinct culturally grounded systems of authority share jurisdiction over the same behaviors their coparticipation in managing offenses may lessen the control effectiveness of both systems.

The assumption of responsibility over a community by outside agencies in ways which ignore or contradict cultural patterns by which its members delegate authority will generate conflict. It will escalate those conflicts that develop within the jurisdictions of informal community systems of control. The criminal justice system should then recognize different "styles" of control and authority (Nader, 1969).

The frequent incidences of violence bred by police intervention in husband-wife disputes are well-known examples of such jurisdictional tension (Lundsgaarde, 1977). It would be difficult to argue, however, that most American minority communities offer structures of authority and exchange analogous in strength to those of many American nuclear families. There are, unfortunately, few detailed ethnographic accounts of cultural groups in American urban settings which examine cultures through the views of their adherents. As Stack (1974) states, statistical patterns are not cultural patterns. In addition, popular evolutionary perspectives assume that community level control mechanisms have, in general, broken down as other types of institutions have assumed greater responsibility in the arena of problem solving. Stack (1974: 22) claims, "Few studies of the black family in the United States have highlighted either the adaptive strategies, resourcefulness, and resilience of urban families under conditions of perpetual poverty or the stability of their kin networks."

Stack lived for three years with Black families in "The Flats," the poorest section of a Black community in a midwestern city. Her findings suggest that evolutionary assumptions which associate mobility with community breakdown are too generally and broadly applied to American cities.

Stack found that some families do move out of the Flats as they accumulate capital or respond to economic opportunity. They generally move, however, to escape the rigid community system of social control, for the glue of control in The Flats lies in the sharing of goods and services. Although the move robs the community of needed resources, it does not weaken extant control mechanisms.

Stack charted extensive stable networks of cooperating kinsmen in The Flats. Those networks encompass from 70 to 300 residents involved in various coalitions of kinsmen. The extensive nature of cooperating networks of kin is facilitated by a flexible cultural connotation of kin which does not confine kin positions to relatives by blood or marriage.

Essentially, when friends in The Flats more than adequately share in customary exchanges of goods and services, they achieve the position of kinsman. Kinsman, here, is what Goodenough (1970: 24) refers to as a "jural role," one which can be identified cross-culturally "not by its content but by some constant among the criteria by which people are entitled to the role," (Stack, 1974: 87).

Achieving the position of kinsman and participating in the customary exchange system are integrated by the transfer of authority over children between friends and the conjugal family. Although authority over children is allocated to individuals who are not kin, that authority is assumed and acted out within the idiom of kinship.

Participation in kin-friend mutual-aid networks requires a strong commitment to the customary system. "Friends can ask any favor of one another, any time of the night, and it shouldn't make any difference," (Stack, 1974: 21).

Stack states that the extensive cooperative system among Black families and friends in The Flats has evolved as one which involves "patterns of co-residence, kinship based exchange networks linking multiple domestic units, elastic household boundaries, and lifelong bonds to three generational households," (1974: 124).

Residents of The Flats clearly operate within two different systems in relation to issues involving their children: their community-based customary system which relates the transfer of authority to the exchange of goods and services and the official legal system of the courts and welfare agencies (Stack, 1974: 46). And, as would be expected, efforts by outside agencies to interfere in issues related to children are successfully resisted by domestic groups in The Flats (Stack, 1974: 89).

Stack's research, and her acceptance as a White woman into Black kin networks, illustrates three important dynamics of Flat social control:

(1) There are extensive kin networks characterized by high commitment. Membership may be achieved in these networks through the transfer of authority which is directly associated with continued economic exchange behavior.

(2) There are strong cultural patterns which dictate behaviors which must be associated with authority roles, thus confining authority to multiplex relationships entailing specific exchange obligations.

(3) Although the authority of outsiders over residents of The Flats may be legitimized by the law or bureaucratic charter, the authority of outsiders will not be viewed as legitimate by Flats residents unless it also involves participation in the customary local system of control.

Flats residents attach to the jural role of authority criteria which are not recognized within the control systems of the larger society. Similarly, the criteria by which outside systems justify their authority are not sufficient to legitimize their authority over or within Flats social relations. Cross-cultural legal research on encapsulated cultures, such as The Flats, suggests that violation by outsiders of customary community boundaries and styles of authority are likely to be resisted, may result in the entrenchment of cultural differences, will not successfully control target behaviors or offenses, and may generate violence across cultural boundaries (Parnell, 1978b).

Examination of patterns of control and authority distribution in The Flats suggests that it need not be the absence of a strong organization of control but, rather, its presence which may generate status-based offenses. The organization of large numbers of people into multistranded relationships based on rights and duties defined clearly within the idiom of kinship provides, as Lundsgaarde (1977) suggests in his examination of homicide in Houston, a fertile ground for violation of status-based obligations. This social potential for offenses may be lessened, however, by the option the kinship system provides to leave a status by not participating in exchange behavior, thus allowing status reciprocals to avoid interpersonal conflicts.

It is perhaps the broader structural factor, the encapsulation of the Black kinship/authority system within a larger system of authority legitimized by different criteria, which is more responsible for generating conflict (1) across the customary boundaries of the community when intervention by outsiders violates them and (2) as a result of the weakening impact of culture conflict on outside authorities as viable alternatives in cooling community conflicts.

THE PROBLEM OF AUTHORITY, PROCESS, AND EXTERNALITIES

Recognizing that cultural differences may generate conflict when outsiders attempt to impose their views on a community, Danzig (1973) has proposed changing the structure of criminal justice systems in order to lessen imbalances in recognition of culturally grounded norms. He refers to the problems as one of "externalities," the imposition of one group's norms on a different group through the coercive mechanisms of the criminal justice system.

The problem of externalities is also generated by the bureaucracies through which law is enforced. The enforcement of state and municipal structures of authority by individuals in bureaucratic positions subjects law to the influence of customs developed within bureaucracies. Even if there were not historical or economic bases for cultural differences among American groups, those groups underrepresented within bureaucratic positions, such as The Flats, would be disenfranchised by the influence of bureaucratic custom over law enforcement activities.

Spradley (1970), Mileski (1971), Parnell (1978a), and others have documented how bureaucratic structures staffed by professionals generate norms which mediate between law and law enforcement.

Conflicts are generated not only by the normative differences among cultural groups which are clearly demarcated by race, ethnicity, historical experience, and geography but also by differences among the processes through which social control is affected on local, municipal, and state levels of law. Following Montesquieu's lead, we would attempt to achieve justice in law enforcement by reaching for the most effective fit among all processes of control in a cultural or social setting. An effective fit would generate the least amount of conflict among styles of authority and processes of dispute settlement.

Finding such a fit in The Flats would involve putting together a very intricate puzzle. The pieces would be norms of the law and norms of the community; norms of bureaucracies and the community; and norms of professionals and those of Flats residents. To compound the task, a fit would have to be found among the processes and styles generated by a kinship structure and those generated by bureaucratic structures. The alternative to fitting these factors together analytically is establishing a flexible larger structure of control through which participants in control can peacefully assert and compromise their differences.

Danzig (1973) suggests managing the absence of coordination among systems of control in New York City through decentralization of the criminal justice system. His plan involves authority sharing among criminal justice officials and community residents who would act as the functional equivalents of police, judges, prosecutors, and legislators. All role players would be responsive to community norms and styles and, through their easy access and direct accountability as residents, would translate the views of the community into the processes of law enforcement.

Some other alternatives to state law and bureaucratic processes are presently operating in American cities under the auspices of the Neighborhood Justice Centers Program in the U.S. Department of Justice (McGillis and Mullen, 1977). These alternatives provide mediation, arbitration, and community support as alternatives to the mediation and adjudication of disputes by the police and courts.

Mediation appears to be a promising process for the compromising of differences. The very nature of the process of mediation legitimizes the pragmatic concerns of community residents and helps them to manage their conflicts of interest, the problems and ambiguities in their relationships, and interpersonal problems which could escalate because of the absence of a third party not backed by coercive force.

The preliminary findings of McGillen and Mullen (1977) are that experiments with mediation and arbitration programs staffed by community residents have been successful in cooling and managing conflicts without the involvement of official criminal justice agencies.

However, neither Danzig nor the Neighborhood Criminal Justice Centers evaluators consider, in their proposals and evaluation, the impact of decentralization and/or the proferring of alternatives on authority relations among groups. The official organization of community-based alternatives, other community mechanisms of control, and the criminal justice system into a system of appeals increases the importance of finding the most effective fit among those systems of control. An official community-municipality-state system of appeals would indeed highlight their stylistic and procedural differences. The appeals system would provide a structure in which conflicts inherent to the different authority structures would be acted out, but not necessarily managed or resolved.

Both the Neighborhood Justice Centers and the community criminal justice systems which are part of Danzig's proposal share jurisdictions with official criminal justice systems. Parties may appeal their cases from alternatives to agencies of the official system or they may bypass the alternatives in favor of other agencies. Under Danzig's proposal, community residents may call on municipal police and courts instead of or in addition to their community counterparts.

Danzig (1973) points out that appeal from the community to the formal system of control must be maintained to check abuses of authority, or the violation of citizens' rights, during community-level processing of disputes.

Anthropologists have described systems of law which, in comparison to the United States, are decentralized. These systems organize local customary and state processes of dispute settlement into a common system of appeals (cf. Canter, 1978; Ruffini, 1978; Witty, 1978; Bailey, 1960; Buxbaum, 1967; Elias, 1963; Nader and Metgzer, 1963; Parnell 1978a). Several of those systems involve, like those proposed for and in operation in the United States, mediation and state-level adjudication of disputes. The dynamics of those systems, though peculiar to their particular social, cultural, and economic settings, offer examples of the types of dynamics which may develop among authority structures such as kinship systems, communities, and state bureaucratic legal systems when all are organized into the same structure of law. The following provides a glimpse at a Mexican version of this type of decentralized legal system.

COMPETITION IN COMMUNITY CONTROL

Competition dominates relations between the state and village in the state system of appeals in the judicial district of Villa Nueva, Oaxaca, Mexico (Parnell, 1978b). On the local level, village court officials are elected and police are appointed and all are responsible to the village and local custom rather than the state and its written codes. Village officials most frequently mediate disputes, although they do adjudicate some disputes when mediation, in the long run, fails or when a combination of both processes is effective in managing a particular dispute. Either the disputants or court officials may appeal a dispute to a district-level state court. In state courts, disputes are adjudicated by judges appointed by the state. Individuals with and without law degrees rise to the position of judge by working within the state legal system. These judges respond to state law rather than local custom.

The predominant view in the village is that the state should not be allowed the authority to interfere in village affairs, even though the customary village legal systems are organized by law into the state system of appeals. In order to resist the state, and to control its participation in local affairs, villagers have infused local social control processes with strategies of political control. Village strategies of resistance are applied, in part, as a response to violations by state criminal justice officials of customary views of authority and jurisdiction during state investigations of cases, including those sent to the state by village court officials.

Strategies of competition change the processes of both the state and the village. The state achieves closure in only a few of the cases it opens. When villages and/or individual villagers do not cooperate with a state-level investigation and hearing, district-level state court officials rely on gossip which their personal contacts can provide them. This gossip may be of a political nature and may have little or nothing to do with incidents related to the offense under investigation. State court official use of personal contacts for information results in inequitable access to the judicial process.

Competition changes the style of village control processes. The threat of the use of coercive force by village officials becomes greater as they attempt to prevent disputants from challenging their authority by appealing cases to the district-level state court. Disputes which would have been mediated are adjudicated. This change creates an imbalance in the relationships among village social control mechanisms, for the general style of village dispute settlement is to repair relationships damaged by an offense rather than, as in adjudication, to determine the guilt or innocence of a disputant and then coerce a disputant to accept a decision.

Village court officials also fabricate investigations of cases which they are required to send to the district-level state court in appealed cases. The fabrication prevents the state from interfering in local management of actual disputes.

Not all villages are equally successful in resisting state legal efforts, for the formulation and implementation of strategies is directly tied to village organization.

The origins of village populations, the degree of dualism and stratification in village structure, the level of villager migration, the strength and style of village leadership, and historical/developmental factors influence the abilities of residents of different villages to resist state court investigations and the frequency with which they appeal disputes to the state.

The fit between the state bureaucratic system of law and different village organizations results, then, in variations in the participation of the state in village control and in the response state participation generates. Cultural and stylistic conflict exists between the village community, state law, and state law enforcers. The overlapping of village/state jurisdictions of control and their organizations into a common system of appeals introduces cultural and stylistic conflict into the dispute settlement processes of both systems. Variations in the fit between state and village structures result in variations in village competition and cooperation with the state as stylistic and cultural conflicts are acted out in the settlement of specific disputes.

The operation of the appeals system in the Mexican decentralized system merely focuses attention on the fact that the fit between community and state control mechanisms will influence the nature of control processes and the success of the legal system in managing disputes. Similar dynamics may inevitably develop in those systems in the United States fostered by decentralization and which share jurisdiction with the criminal justice system. This possibility does not argue against decentralization. Community-level control processes will continue to operate with or without official recognition. The absence of official recognition may indeed strengthen those processes as well as the strategies of avoidance and resistance which they incorporate. Rather, the Mexican experience argues for decentralization through considered planning, recognition of the force of environmental factors on the processes of law, and the creation of an appeals system styled to manage conflicts among cultural groups and community interests.

ENGINEERING COMMUNITY CONTROL

Engineering for community control may necessitate the building of new structures of law and the introduction of new concepts of legal jurisdiction. How is it possible to minimize the conflicts that overlapping jurisdictions may entail and yet maintain vigilance over abuses that may arise within community-controlled systems?

A parallel approach to judicial design on community and official levels may provide a potential answer to this question.

The assignment of sole jurisdiction to community systems over the types of conflicts they can most effectively manage would lessen the effect of jurisdictional conflicts. It would decrease the potential of conflict across boundaries of authority resulting from outside violation of customary authority patterns.

The restructuring of jurisdictions requires, first of all, the creation of dispute/dispute settlement typologies, ones which relate types of disputes to the processes which can most effectively manage them. Analyses of disputing behavior by Gulliver (1973), Felstiner (1974), Gibbs (1963), Witty (n.d.), Nader (1978), Canter (1978), and Ruffini (1978) provide a well-documented basis for such a typology. These researchers examine the fit between such processes as mediation, negotiation, and adjudication; the structural/and organizational environments in which they develop and operate; and the types of disputes which they seem to most effectively manage and/or resolve.

Most important, the typology of dispute settlement should be subjected to close examination of its application in the United States. For example, the cross-cultural literature suggests that mediation arises in situations in which the repairing of relationships between disputants is more important than determining guilt and innocence. This suggests that mediation will be most effective in managing interpersonal conflicts. However, Witty (n.d.) and Mullen and McGillis (1977) have shown that mediation can be effective in dealing with a much wider range of disputes.

The setting of dispute settlement may be as important as the process. A third-party mediator or adjudicator will be much more effective if his or her authority is accepted by the parties to a dispute. Merely taking settlement responsibility out of the hands of authorities whose jural roles are legitimized by the force of the state rather than community or cultural criteria will infuse settlement processes with a sense of order rather than adversity.

The criteria of effectiveness must be grounded in the views of the regulated. Goals in dispute settlement and the adequacy of solutions are culturally specific. A typology of dispute settlement can thus not achieve adequacy solely on the basis of logical analysis. Legal engineers must do what legal officials have failed to do: integrate the customs of the regulated into the law and its enforcement processes. Mediation, for example, may not be successful across status relations, such as those in The Flats, which entail a clear-cut distribution of authority which cannot be compromised without challenging cultural expectations.

Community-based alternatives may be able to deal effectively with intragroup disputes when their jurisdiction over those disputes is not challenged, but what about those conflicts which arise in more heterogeneous communities among different groups and those between residents of different communities? A decentralized system may, in strengthening communities, also strengthen community differences. Assignment of sole jurisdiction to communities over certain behaviors provides no recourse to residents victimized by others who abuse community control.

Appeal to municipal and state courts may punish abusers within specific cases, but it will not manage the situation which gives rise to abuse. Adjudication of appealed disputes that arise within and among communities will likely strengthen their differences and escalate the conflict if parties and their associates have no choice but to continue their interactions. Avoidance of relationships, whether it is imposed by or results from municipal or state legal actions, as a pattern, parodies the goals of community control.

An alternative to the first instance of appeals, one which lies between community and official control systems, could mediate in those areas of authority conflict where the goals of the community and the goals of the state are inimical. As a regional alternative, it could also mediate inter- and intracommunity conflicts which have cultural and stylistic origins. It could provide third parties, drawn from community residents, who could manage an arena of confrontation in which differences among and within communities could be faced before they escalate into the types of interpersonal and intergroup conflicts which are difficult to resolve without resorting to the extremes of avoidance and/or coercive force.

The composition and style of the alternative first instance of appeals should be engineered to be representative of the communities involved. The regional alternative would extend the goals of community control to the integration of control processes extant within the American groups and institutions.

CONCLUSIONS

A number of cultural factors specific to communities may influence whether their residents react through indifference, conformity, acceptance, or resistance to outside control processes. Foremost among these are customs which influence the designation of jural roles, processes which influence the assumption and acting out of jural roles, styles of authority and community control processes, and the general structures of communities and controllers as they influence the organization of internal and intergroup control. Giving greater responsibility and jurisdiction in control to communities such as The Flats may eliminate conflicts of authority, style, and structure which result from the involvement of the official criminal justice system in community problems. But community-based justice may strengthen conflicts when they are latent or manifest in other arenas of intergroup relations. Cultural conflict may be managed most effectively through coupling community-based justice with the establishment of an alternative structure of appeals flexible enough to mediate between intercommunity conflicts and conflicts between community residents and state and municipal bureaucrats.

REFERENCES

Bailey, F. G. (1960) *Tribe, Caste and Nation*. Manchester, England: Manchester University Press.

Buxbaum, D. C. (1967) *Traditional and Modern Legal Institutions in Asia and Africa*. Leiden, The Netherlands: E. J. Brill.

Canter, R. (1978) "Dispute settlement and dispute processing in Zambia: Individual choice versus societal constraints" pp. 247-280 in L. Nader and H. F. Todd, Jr. (eds.) *The Disputing Process—Law in Ten Societies*. New York: Columbia University Press.

Danzig, R. (1973) "Toward the creation of a complementary decentralized system of criminal justice." *Stanford Law Review*, 26: 1-54.

Elias, T. O. (1963) *The Nigerian Legal System*. London: Routledge and Kegan Paul.

Felstiner, W. F. (1974) "Influences of social organization on dispute processing." *Law and Society Review*, 9: 63-94.

Goodenough, W. (1970) *Description and Comparison in Cultural Anthropology*. Chicago: Aldine.

Gibbs, J. L. (1963) "The Kpelle moot: A therapeutic model for the informal settlement of disputes." *Africa*, 33: 1-11.

Gulliver, P. H. (1973) Negotiation as a mode of dispute settlement: Towards a general model." *Law and Society Review,* 7: 667-691.

Lewis, O. (1959) *Five Families: Mexican Case Studies in the Culture of Poverty.* New York: Basic Books.

Lundsgaarde, H. P. (1977) *Murder in Space City: A Cultural Analysis of Houston Homicide Patterns.* New York: Oxford University Press.

Mileski, M. (1971) "Courtroom encounters: An observation study of a lower criminal court." *Law and Society Review,* 5: 473-538.

Nader, L. (1969) "Styles of court procedure: To make the balance," pp. 69-91 in L. Nader (ed.) *Law in Culture and Society.* Chicago: Aldine.

——— and D. Metzger (1963) "Conflict resolution in two Mexican communities." *American Anthropologist,* 65: 484-492.

Nader, L. and H. F. Todd, Jr. (1978) *The Disputing Process—Law in Ten Societies.* New York: Columbia University Press.

Parnell, P. C. (1978a) "Village or state? Competitive legal systems in a Mexican judicial district," pp. 315-350 in L. Nader and H. F. Todd, Jr. (eds.) *The Disputing Process—Law in Ten Societies.* New York: Columbia University Press.

——— (1978b) "Conflict and competition in a Mexican judicial district." (unpublished)

Pospisil, L. (1971) *Anthropology of Law: A Comparative Theory.* New York: Harper & Row.

Ruffini, J. L. (1978) "Disputing over livestock in Sardinia," pp. 209-246 in L. Nader and H. F. Todd, Jr. (eds.) *The Disputing Process—Law in Ten Societies.* New York: Columbia University Press.

Spradley, J. P. (1970) *You Owe Yourself a Drunk: An Ethnography of Urban Nomads.* Boston: Little, Brown.

Stack, C. (1974) *All Our Kin: Strategies for Survival in a Black Community.* New York: Harper & Row.

Witty, C. J. (forthcoming) *Mediation and Society: Conflict Management in Lebanon.* New York: Academic Press.

——— (1978) "Disputing issues in Shehaam, a multireligious village in Lebanon," pp. 281-314 in L. Nader and H. F. Todd, Jr. (eds.) *The Disputing Process—Law in Ten Societies.* New York: Columbia University Press.

9

CRIMINOLOGY AND CRIMINAL JUSTICE EDUCATION IN HISTORICALLY BLACK COLLEGES AND UNIVERSITIES

Julius Debro

Atlanta University

INTRODUCTION

Criminology and criminal justice education, as a discipline in most historically black colleges and universities, is a recent phenomenon occurring largely within the last 10 years. Presently there are fewer than 20 programs in over 100 postsecondary black institutions. In contrast, predominantly white institutions have over 1300 programs. White institutions had very few programs prior to the early 1960s but after the riots programs proliferated at a rapid pace. This can be attributed to federal moneys' being offered by the Law Enforcement Assistance Administration (LEAA).

In 1967, the President's Commission on Law Enforcement and Administration of Justice called on the nation's police departments to "establish a minimum requirement of a baccalaureate degree for all supervisory and executive positions." The call was later echoed by the National Advisory Commission on Civil Disorders and by the National Advisory Commission on Criminal Justice Standards and Goals. In a response to these calls for higher education for police officers, LEAA began to offer moneys to police departments so that the officers could augment their education.

Predominantly white universities moved swiftly to obtain these funds for the training of police. Black colleges and universities did not respond and thus were not beneficiaries of the new moneys provided by the federal government for police education. There are three explanations for the lack of participation by black colleges. These include: (1) a lack of knowledge by black colleges and universities regarding how to obtain the necessary funds; (2) a lack of commitment by LEAA to mention specifically black colleges and universities in their comprehensive plans; and (3) there were very few black police officers to educate in most police departments throughout the country.

It is highly probable that all three of the above explanations contributed to the lack of criminal justice programs in black colleges. Black administrators of the colleges, until recently, have not been acutely aware of funding possibilities within LEAA. There was no specific commitment to assist black colleges in establishing programs in criminal justice. It was not until 1973 that the Office of Criminal Justice Education and Training (within LEAA) specifically indicated an interest in funding historical black colleges. The harbinger of that interest was the development of a criminal justice education program for black colleges (both ongoing and developing) by an organization called Positive Futures Incorporated. Even then it was not until 1975 that the Office of Criminal Justice Education and Training funded its first proposal which was specifically designed to assist black colleges in developing criminal justice programs.

Nine years later, attempts are finally being made to rectify the nation's noncommitment to historical black colleges and universities. Along these lines, President Carter issued a memorandum on January 17, 1979, to all Executive Departments and agencies which stated in part that each agency should conduct a thorough review of the operations within their departments to insure that historical black institutions are being given a fair opportunity to participate in federal grant and contract programs. It appears that the government finally has recognized that the awarding of grants and contracts is still not being equitably distributed throughout the country.

This article summarizes the early history since 1908 of criminology and criminal justice education, presents an overview of criminology and criminal justice education, presents an overview of criminology and criminal justice programs as they currently exist in historically black colleges, and finally specifies some alternatives aimed at improving the quality of criminology and criminal justice education in historically black colleges and universities.

HISTORICAL DEVELOPMENT OF
CRIMINAL JUSTICE EDUCATION

August Vollmer, former Town Marshall of Berkeley, California, is considered by most scholars to be the founder of criminology and criminal justice education in America. In 1908, Vollmer saw the need for a program of education which would provide additional knowledge for police officers who were working with the public on a day-to-day basis. He believed that police should not only be trained in police techniques but should also be formally educated as well. One year later, Northwestern University convened a national conference on criminal law and criminology (Brandstatter, 1973; Farris, 1972; Foster, 1974). This conference was the first recorded involvement of higher education in the criminal justice field. During the conference, the following three resolutions were adopted which shaped the formulation of programs and education for the next decade:

(1) establishment of the American Institute of Criminal Law and Criminology
(2) initiation of publication in 1910 of the *Journal of Criminal Law, Criminology and Police Science*
(3) translation into English of the significant volumes on criminology authored by foreign scholars [Stephens, 1976].

In 1911, police training programs were developed in Detroit and in 1914 in New York, but the next academic program was not initiated until 1925 at Northwestern University. In 1929, a major program was developed at the University of Chicago. This program was important because it was the first degree-granting program in crime-related studies to be housed in a political science department (Fabian, cited in Foster, 1974: 32).

Programs were developed during the 1930s at San Jose State, Michigan State, Indiana University, and the University of Washington. There were very few programs developed during the 1940s and 1950s, but in the 1960s there was a massive influx of programs. California's two-year colleges lead the way in providing criminology and criminal justice degree programs. The programs in the California two-year colleges were considered to be quite good but, since that time, two-year colleges have been subjected to criticism primarily in the area of faculty selection.

TABLE 1   Criminal Justice Academic Programs

Directory	Associate	Baccalaurate	Masters	Ph.D	# Institutions
1964-1965	80	32	20	7	97
1966-1967	152	39	14	4	184
1968-1969	199	44	13	5	234
1970-1971	257	55	21	7	292
1972-1973	505	211	41	9	515
1975-1976	729	376	121	19	664

SOURCE: IACP Directories 1965-75.

Since 1965, the International Association of Chiefs of Police (IACP) has maintained records of programs. Table 1 indicates the number of educational programs that have been identified. There are presently over 1300 programs in criminology and criminal justice throughout the nation (Joint Commission on Criminology and Criminal Justice Education, 1979).

THE RISE OF LEAA AND CRIMINAL JUSTICE EDUCATION

The primary reason for the current proliferation of criminal justice and criminology educational programs should be attributed to the Black population, yet they have not been the beneficiaries of these programs. If it had not been for the riots of the 1960s, legislation would not have been passed creating the Law Enforcement Assistance Act of 1965 and the Omnibus Crime Control and Safe Streets Act of 1968.

One of the single most important factors in the proliferation of Criminal Justice Higher Education programs has been in the increased federal funding first made available by the Law Enforcement Assistance Act in 1965 (Public Law 89-197) and then by the Omnibus Crime Control and Safe Streets Act of 1968 (Public Law 90-351). The Law Enforcement Assistance Act created the Office of Law Enforcement Assistance (OLEA) that started a program of small grants to help develop and implement Police Science Degree Programs.

The Omnibus Crime Control and Safe Streets Act then created the Law Enforcement Assistance Administration (LEAA), which was authorized to underwrite programs of academic financial assistance [National Manpower Survey, 1978].

Essentially, LEAA was created to deal with "Black Lawlessness" of the 1960s. It responded in the following five years by equipping police departments with riot control gear and related hardware (for which LEAA was severely criticized). In addition, LEAA funded undergraduate and graduate degree programs for police in white universities which only served to reinforce Black-white antagonisms within this country. For the most part, police attitudes did not change as a result of education.

Blacks perceived the criminal justice system as discriminatory. They also felt that increasing the education requirements of white policemen could not significantly impact on a system that already had white policemen, white judges, white jailers, and white correctional personnel. Blacks were aware that racial prejudice has always been part of the system and were not optimistic enough to believe that police prejudice would be reduced by education. As Silberman has stated, "there is no reason why the police should be exempt from the prejudice that afflicts every group in American society" (Silberman, 1978: 43).

The National Advisory Commission on Higher Education for police officers found that the present structure of police education as taught in postsecondary schools often resulted "in little more than tacking credit on to police personnel, and serving the status quo in policing rather than stimulating change" (National Advisory Commission on Higher Education, 1979). Although there were no specific recommendations for the above statement, perhaps it does serve to show that institutions of higher learning were doing little to bring about change in police thought and behavior. Even if colleges were successful in changing attitudes, policemen, upon returning to their departments, returned to racist organizational milieus and to traditional methods of policing (Silberman, 1978).

BLACK COLLEGES RESPONSE TO CRIMINOLOGY AND CRIMINAL JUSTICE PROGRAMS

When discussing the black colleges' and universities' response to criminology and criminal justice programs, three definitive areas must be recognized. These three areas include the black college administrator, prospective faculty, and student recruitment.

Administrators

Black administrators, for the most part, did not embrace criminology and criminal justice educational programs that had as a basis of support Law Enforcement Education and Planning funding. Black administrators were aware that in the past they had received only the crumbs from the tables of this nation's educational funds and they were concerned that this would merely be a continuation of that pattern. This has been true whether these funds have been provided by corporations, church bodies, government, or foundations (e.g., eight traditionally white universities were funded by LEAA at a level in excess of $1 million for three years to establish Ph.D. programs, yet less than $1 million was given to nine black schools to establish a bachelor's program). Black colleges and universities have been fighting for their very existence within the last two decades. Starting new programs when most schools were running a deficit did not seem cost effective.

Faculty

Faculty selection was perhaps the most burning issue among black administrators. There were just not sufficient numbers of Blacks with terminal degrees who could establish programs and teach students. In 1979, there were only nine Blacks with terminal degrees in criminology and criminal justice in the entire nation. Moreover, there are only five Blacks with terminal degrees teaching at colleges and universities (three are teaching at historical black colleges and two are teaching at predominantly white universities). The field has not been able to sell itself to bright young scholars primarily because of the negative image that criminal justice carries within the Black community.

Students

There has been a continuous fight to enroll black students at most historically black institutions. The reason for this is clear. White institutions of higher education are making it more and more attractive for black students to attend their universities. Financial packages have been worked out at predominantly white universities specifically to recruit black students. For example, State University of New York at Albany has a three-year package worked out with LEAA to recruit minorities into its criminal justice program. The University of Maryland, at College Park, also has such a program.

How will black colleges and universities be able to attract black students in sufficient numbers to support such programs? There is no ready answer to this question. There was also the belief held by black college administrators and black criminal justice academicians that black students simply have not been interested in perpetuating a criminal justice system that has been racist in the past in its approach to black crime problems and to black offenders. Whether criminal justice education has perpetuated racist beliefs is not the issue. The issue is that black students perceived and still do perceive the system to be discriminatory. In light of these issues, will education, even at black colleges and universities, make a difference?

Increasingly more Black middle-class parents now send their children to white institutions because they believe those institutions to offer better education than historically black colleges and universities. The perception of a better education in white institutions in some cases is true, but there is a more fundamental question of the uniqueness of black colleges and universities. The "minority perspective" that black pupils need and should receive is absent particularly in criminal justice programs at white institutions. Most black youngsters upon graduation will return to a Black environment, not so much by choice but by design. They need to know not only the social problems that exist within black communities but also the reason for the existence of these problems.

In white universities, the majority perspective is the dominant theme. In criminology and criminal justice, that dominant theme is a conservative one which often conflicts with Black themes of social justice. French describes the conservative theme in criminal justice in this manner:

> The criminal justice perspective in the United States is a socially conservative one supportive of the white male (WASP) practitioners who comprise the Administration of Justice. Clearly, this perspective supports its own self-fulfilling myopic, prophecy. J. Edgar Hoover, Bull Conners and Frank Rizzo are criminal justice personalities who illustrate this phenomenon. Consequently, it is to no one's surprise to find that this orientation has found itself into the classrooms of

our nation's community colleges, colleges and universities, especially those which jumped on the bandwagon and established special "Criminal Justice programs to qualify for monies [French, 1979: 4].

Despite the conservative perspective, black students are gravitating more and more to white universities. The gravitation began with the influx of scholarship moneys and will continue for some time to come even though the dominant theme remains conservative. The end result is that black schools find it more difficult to recruit outstanding black students. In the future, we will not be able to look to black colleges and universities for outstanding students such as the late Reverend Dr. Martin Luther King, Jr., Andrew Young, and Maynard Jackson, because outstanding students now attend predominantly white universities.

Black students today can be classified into three distinct categories:

(1) the *outstanding* young scholar who is *middle class* and will generally obtain his or her education at one of the more prestigious white colleges or universities.

(2) the *above average* student who is a product of the *lower middle class* but elects to remain within his or her own state and obtain an education from the state university.

(3) the *average or marginal student* who has decided to attend one of the historical black institutions primarily because of low grades and secondarily because of a commitment to black institutions.

The separation of black students into these categories is not absolute but it does reflect an identifiable trend at the undergraduate and graduate level. Certainly there are still students who excell and simply decide to enter black institutions because they are seeking a positive black identity which cannot be found on white campuses, but they are increasingly rare. There are also excellent students who attend black colleges and universities simply because their parents attended those universities and there is a tradition within the family that holds to better education at black institutions.

Despite the enrollment problem in general, black students appear to be entering the fields of public administration, sociology, business administration, psychology, and related disciplines. Another reason for their failure to enter the field of criminal justice may be that there are so few role models in the criminal justice system. In the corrections field, there is only one black director of corrections in the country. In the judicial field, there are very few judges, court reporters, clerks, or bailiffs who are black. Within State Planning Agencies (arms of LEAA), blacks are even less visible. In fact, there are only two blacks that head State Planning Agencies throughout the country. In the police sector, blacks are represented at a much higher level in managerial positions than in any other area. While there are numerous chiefs, with few exceptions they are located in major cities with black-controlled city governments.

Prospective black students see that our prisons and jails are filled with blacks but see very few black administrators within the system, thus concluding that the system is institutionally segregated and will remain so regardless of their presence. Black students do not wish to be caretakers of a system that has a history of discriminatory treatment of blacks from arrest through release.

Some black students are entering criminology and criminal justice programs but their numbers are few. While there are approximately 100 black colleges and universities, only 15 have some form of a criminal justice program. Further, most of those programs, as in white institutions, are housed within other departments and only provide a specialty in criminology and/or criminal justice.

At the undergraduate level, LEAA has funded Positive Futures, Inc. (PFI) to provide technical assistance to nine black colleges which either had programs or were in the process of establishing programs. These schools include Grambling in Louisiana; Shaw in Detroit; Shaw in North Carolina; Talladega in Alabama; Texas Southern in Texas; Bishop in Texas; Miles in Alabama; Mississippi Valley in Mississippi; and Fayetteville in North Carolina. Technical assistance and start-up moneys, though somewhat meager, were provided for those universities and colleges to establish an undergraduate program. With the exception of Miles, all of these programs are or will be completely supported by their respective colleges and universities rather than depend on government funding. Among the black colleges, three schools (Lincoln University in Missouri, Jackson State University in Mississippi, and Bishop College in Texas) have the oldest criminal justice programs.

The original funding of PFI had as the intent to test whether increased cooperation, coordination, and communication would facilitate the effective development of a mutually supportive network of service delivery among the participating institutions (Positive Futures, Inc., 1979). Each criminal justice program was to fully meet the accreditation standards of the Academy of Criminal Justice Sciences.

TABLE 2   Student Enrollment

Institution	Total No. Students
Bishop College	1,375
Grambling	3,639
Fayetteville	2,125
Talladega	704
Miles	1,146
Shaw University	1,267
Shaw College	805
Texas Southern Univ.	8,556
Winston-Salem State	2,304

A recent survey by PFI of the above nine schools indicated that there were 851 students and 28 faculty in the nine programs. The average age of the students was 33.9 and the average age of the faculty 30.5 years. Additionally, based on interviews with the students, the report indicated that a majority would recommend the criminal justice degree programs to their friends but they did suggest the following improvements:

(1) hiring more and better-prepared instructors
(2) providing better facilities and classrooms
(3) offering more courses
(4) recruiting a broader cross-section of students
(5) providing more and better library facilities
(6) providing students with more field experiences and guest lecturers.

Table 2 gives some indication of the total student enrollment of the schools involved in the project.

Most of the schools have small enrollments and understandably were concerned with the initiation of new programs because it reduced the student enrollment of other programs. Yet, after three years, the PFI consortium schools were pleased that they had initiated Criminology and Criminal Justice programs.

The final review of these programs indicated that:

(1) The initial level of financial support was not adequate to operation-
    alize project objectives.
(2) The original project concept appeared to be overly ambitious.
(3) The institutional commitment to project excellence could have
    been better.

The conclusion of the report indicated that the programs were organized and managed "in a manner that supports service delivery and cost
effectiveness" (Positive Futures, Inc., 1979).

Most of the Black schools follow the identical core curriculum that is
standard throughout the field including such courses as·

(1) Introduction to Law Enforcement
(2) Introduction to the Criminal Justice System
(3) Introduction to Corrections
(4) Introduction to Criminology
(5) Criminal Court Procedures
(6) Criminal and Legal Aspects of Law Enforcement and Corrections.

The difference in the above core curriculum as taught in black colleges
and Universities is that most of the instructors introduce the black perspective, using black authors to supplement readings within the field. Most
white universities are not aware of the writings of black authors and do
not make attempts to locate their writings (Debro, 1978).

Prior to 1978, there were no Criminology or Criminal Justice Educational programs at the graduate level in black colleges. Efforts have been
made to establish such a graduate program at Howard University in
Washington, D.C., but because of the administration's reluctance to provide departmental status to such a program, it has thus far been unsuccess-
ful. LEAA provided substantial funding to establish such a program and
the university recruited a Black professor from Portland State University
to be its organizer but after two years of frustration caused mainly by the
faculty being unable to accept the field as an academic discipline, the
professor resigned and returned to Portland.

Another Black professor has continued the fight at Howard University to establish a program but also has met with resistance and does not see that a Criminal Justice Department will be a reality in the future because of the split among the sociology faculty who would like the program to be a part of sociology and not a department of its own.

Atlanta University has just established a Master's Degree program in Criminal Justice Administration. Atlanta is seeking to move beyond just a mere program in Criminal Justice by attempting to establish a Criminal Justice Institute which will be primarily for the study of Race and Crime.

The institute will have three components: Educational, Research, and Community. The money for the establishment of the institute is being provided by LEAA. The structure for the institute is based upon the necessity of responding to three immediate needs within the criminal justice system:

(1) to increase substantially the pool of black scholars and researchers as well as professionals and community leaders so that they may deal effectively with the problems of crime and crime prevention

(2) to become a center for the study of black crime and criminals and to serve as a repository and clearinghouse for the collection, analysis, and dissemination of all information relating to blacks and crime

(3) to contribute to the upgrading and competencies of Criminal Justice practitioners and providing training programs, seminars and workshops for in-service personnel.

Atlanta University is committed to attracting the best faculty and students regardless of race, creed, color, sex, or national origin. It plans to attract prominent scholars by providing financial as well as housing incentives plus a small faculty-student ratio.

The program at Atlanta will focus primarily on the study of black crime and criminals. It will also provide financial incentives for students as well as assistantships so that students may work directly with well-known professors in the field. Only full-time faculty members with terminal degrees in the discipline or a related discipline will be recruited for the faculty, for it is the faculty members who make the reputation for a given school and faculty possession of terminal degrees to build a national reputation. There are presently 27 students enrolled in the program and it is anticipated that by 1981 there will be no more than 50.

The need to establish more Criminology and Criminal Justice programs within black colleges and universities is a must if we are going to provide a sufficient manpower pool of black educators and practitioners throughout the system. Fifty percent of black students who enter the universities and colleges of this nation attend black institutions yet fewer than 2% of those institutions have Criminology or Criminal Justice programs. White institutions have not been able to meet the need of providing a pool of black practitioners and scholars, so the need continues.

Black colleges should be encouraged to initiate Criminology and Criminal Justice programs not only because they can increase the manpower pool but also because they provide a degree of sensitivity to the causes of black crime and criminals that cannot and has not been provided at white institutions.

Certainly, those programs that have been established at historically black colleges and universities have not been of the best quality. If the quality of criminology and criminal justice programs is going to improve, the following tasks must be completed:

(1) *total commitment by the school administration:* The administration must decide whether it can support a program as it has supported other programs independently of federal dollars. While federal grants should assist a program, programs should not rely entirely upon funding from outside agencies.
(2) *recruit adequate faculty:* Only faculty members with terminal degrees should be recruited. It will be somewhat difficult to recruit persons with terminal degrees in Criminology and Criminal Justice but persons who have degrees in Sociology or other fields that have an emphasis in Criminology or Criminal Justice can be recruited. Programs should be interdisciplinary, thus persons with degrees in allied fields should comprise the total faculty.
(3) *student recruitment:* There must be a more active recruiting effort conducted by black colleges if they expect to compete in the marketplace for good students. Recruitment efforts should not be limited just to black students. Recruitment must include students of all races if black colleges are to survive.

Finally, associations such as the Academy of Criminal Justice Sciences and the American Society of Criminology should provide technical assistance to black colleges and universities, as well as make provisions for Visiting Professor arrangements. Outstanding professors could spend sabbatical leaves at historical black colleges or universities. Such arrangements could promote the exchange of ideas focused upon the resolution of various criminal justice problems, from unique and racially sensitive perspectives.

REFERENCES

Brandstatter, A. F. (1973) "History of police education in U.S.," in *Report of the Standards Committee: Volume II.* Atlanta: Georgia State University.

Brown, L. P. (1974) "The police and higher education: The challenge of the times." *Criminology,* 12: 114-124.

Debro, J. (1979) "Criminology and criminal justice education in predominatly white universities." Presented at the annual meeting of the Academy of Criminal Justice Sciences, Cincinnati, March 14-16.

––– and B. Siman (1978) "Criminology and criminal justice education: Perspectives for the future." Presented at the annual meeting of the American Society of Criminology, Dallas, November 8.

Farris, E. A. (1972) "A history of criminal justice education: Seven decades (1900-1970)," in *Report of the Standard Committee: Volume I.* Atlanta: Georgia State University.

Foster, J. P. (1974) "A descriptive analysis of crime-related programs in higher education. Ph.D. dissertation, Florida State University, Tallahassee.

French, L. (1979) "Teaching the minority perspective in criminal justice." Paper presented at the annual conference of the American Society of Criminology, Philadelphia, November.

Joint Commission on Criminology and Criminal Justice Education and Standards (1978) Report. Washington, DC: Office of Criminal Justice Education and Training.

National Manpower Survey of the Criminal Justice System (1977) *Criminal Justice Education and Training* (Volume 5). Washington, DC: Government Printing Office.

Positive Futures, Inc. (1979) *Final Report, Black Colleges.* Washington, DC: Author.

President's Commission on Law Enforcement and Administration of Justice (1967) *The Challenge of Crime in a Free Society: A Report.* Washington, DC: Government Printing Office.

President's National Advisory Commission on Civil Disorders (1969) Report. Washington, DC: Government Printing Office.

Silberman, C. E. (1978) *Criminal Violence, Criminal Justice.* New York: Random House.

Stephens, G. (1976) "Criminal justice education: Past, present and future." *Criminal Justice Review,* 1: 91-120.

Vollmer, A. and A. Schneider (1917) "A school for police as planned at Berkeley." *Journal of Criminal Law, Criminology and Police Science.*

ABOUT THE AUTHORS

Bonnie J. Bondavalli received her Ph.D. in Sociology, concentrating in criminology and delinquency, from the University of Missouri. She is teaching at Concordia College, River Forest, Illinois.

Bruno Bondavalli is completing a Ph.D. in Bilingual-Bicultural Education at the University of Illinois. He is teaching in a bilingual college program in Chicago.

Tim Bynum received his Ph.D. from Florida State University and is currently Assistant Professor at the School of Criminal Justice at Michigan State University. His prior research has focused upon the impact of extralegal factors upon pretrial release decisions and the police decision to investigate criminal complaints. He is currently engaged in research exploring the fear of crime among college students.

Julius Debro received his Ph.D. of Criminology from the University of California, Berkeley, and is currently chair of the Criminal Justice Administration program at Atlanta University. He has been director and principle investigator of numerous grants focusing on minority issues and has published and presented numerous papers at professional meetings.

William Feyerherm received his Ph.D. in Criminal Justice from the State University of New York at Albany and is currently Assistant Professor with the Criminal Justice Program at the University of Wisconsin—Milwaukee. His research and teaching interests focus upon the measurement of crime, delinquency, research methodology, and statistical analysis.

James J. Fyfe received his Ph.D. in Criminal Justice from the State University of New York at Albany and is currently Associate Professor at the American University School of Justice. He is a former New York City police lieutenant and is a consultant to the Police Foundation. He has published and presented numerous papers dealing with the police use of deadly force.

R. L. McNeely received his Ph.D. from the Heller School for Advanced Studies in Social Welfare, Brandeis University. Currently he is Director, University of Wisconsin—Milwaukee, Center for Adult Development and Associate Professor at the School of Social Welfare. He has presented and published numerous papers in several areas including race and crime, family violence, and the impact of workplace conditions on health and social functioning.

Philip Parnell received his Ph.D. in Anthropology at the University of California, Berkeley, and is currently Assistant Professor of Forensic Studies and Latin American studies at Indiana University in Bloomington. He has conducted research in dispute settlement in Mexico and the United States and teaches in the areas of law, anthropology, and social control.

Carl E. Pope received his Ph.D. in Criminal Justice from the State University of New York at Albany and is currently Associate Professor and Coordinator of the Criminal Justice Graduate Program at the University of Wisconsin—Milwaukee. His research and teaching interests include race and crime, research methodology, criminal justice decision making, and juvenile justice processing.

Richard L. Schuster received his Ph.D. in Sociology from the Ohio State University and is currently Assistant Professor at Virginia Polytechnic Institute and State University. He is coauthor of *The Violent Few*.